Managing
Bank Conversions

Managing
Bank Conversions

*The Guide to Organizing,
Controlling, and Implementing
Systems Conversions*

By Kent S. Belasco

BeardBooks
Washington, D.C.

Copyright © Richard D. Irwin, a Times Mirror Higher Education Group, Inc. 1996
Reprinted 2003 by Beard Books, Washington, D.C.

Library of Congress Cataloging-in-Publication Data

Belasco, Kent S.
    Managing bank conversions : the guide to organizing, controlling, and implementing
systems conversions / by Kent S. Belasco.
        p. cm.
    Originally published: Chicago : Irwin Professional Pub., ©1996.
    Includes bibliographical references and index.
    ISBN: 1-58798-204-8 (pbk. : alk. paper)
        1. Bank investments. 2. Consolidation and merger of corporations. 3. Organizational
change--Management. I. Title.

    HG1616.15B45 2003
    332.1'068'1--dc22

                                                                    2003052398

Printed in the United States of America

This publication is designed to provide accurate and authoritative information in regard
to the subject matter covered. It is sold with the understanding that neither the author nor
the publisher is engaged in rendering legal, accounting, or other professional service. If
legal advice or other expert assistance is required, the services of a competent
professional person should be sought.

— *From a Declaration of Principles jointly adopted by a Committee of the American Bar
Association and a Committee of Publishers*

*To My Friends and Colleagues at First Midwest
for Their Ongoing Support
and Encouragement*

AUTHOR BIOGRAPHY

Kent S. Belasco is the Executive Vice President and Chief Information Officer for First Midwest Bank, N.A., based in Itasca, Illinois. He has held numerous management positions in bank operations, project management and productivity, as well as serving as a consultant to banks and other financial institutions on earnings improvement.

In addition to his B.A. from Lake Forest College and M.B.A. from Lake Forest Graduate School of Management, Mr. Belasco is a Certified Public Accountant, Certified Financial Planner, and a Certified Computer Professional. Currently Mr. Belasco is pursuing a doctoral degree (Ed.D.) in Business Education with a concentration in Management Information Systems at Northern Illinois University.

He is also the author of *Bank Productivity* (Bankers Publishing/Probus, 1990), *Earnings Enhancement Handbook for Financial Institutions* (Bankers Publishing/Probus, 1991), *Analyzing Bank Staffing Levels* (Bankers Publishing/Probus, 1991), and *Bank Systems Management* (Probus Publishing, 1994).

PREFACE

Change has become the latest in a long line of overused buzzwords. Unfortunately, as a result of the present paradigm shift, change is now the norm and will continue to be so in the very near future. The transition from a manufacturing/industrial to an information-based era involves more than the purchase of the latest microcomputer. It is a matter of how one deals with and handles change and takes advantage of the opportunities available from the transition to the next level.

This book is about dealing with, managing, and controlling change. It is about proactively embracing change to capitalize on the opportunities and benefits inherently derived. Alvin Toffler, in his book *Powershift*, stated that information is power. The changes occurring involve information and usage of information. Those organizations who understand this can achieve tremendous breakthrough power and achievement by capitalizing on it. When this occurs, competitive advantages and opportunities can be gained. The way in which change is managed will mark the difference between success and failure. Today, the most successful companies are those most able to deal effectively and efficiently with change. For this reason mergers and acquisitions can represent significant opportunities provided the organization can assimilate the new entity in a timely and effective manner.

This book focuses on what banks must do, operationally, to address and control change effectively and to manage it. The process of converting systems is a phenomenon which has evolved and grown rapidly because of the types and complexity of systems currently deployed. No bank or organization can control the amount and magnitude of changes occurring today without a well organized and structured discipline for managing the change process. Because of the demand and utilization of information and the technology to make the information available, systems will continually be upgraded, enhanced, changed, and replaced. In this regard the process of change becomes a standard, accepted practice.

With the information paradigm shift and the extent of technology available, the world will become increasingly more dynamic. Those able to understand and recognize that change is, or will be, a routine element will be the winners. The net benefit to those organizations will be the ability to move on to the next level and take advantage of the significant business opportunities which become available.

Kent S. Belasco

C O N T E N T S

Introduction   1

Chapter 1

Overview of System Conversion   5

Chapter 2

Organization of the System Conversion   25

LIST OF FIGURES

Introduction

Over the past 10 years U.S. commercial banks have continued to execute bank acquisitions and mergers. It is a trend that, although relatively meager in the last three years or so, is beginning to emerge once again. Recently, major bank acquisitions have occurred that will change the structure and number of commercial banks in this country. For example, most of the larger banks in Illinois have now been acquired by either foreign or out-of-state banking concerns, leaving few large money-center banks that are truly independent. This trend is not likely to dissipate. In conjunction with acquisitions, there usually follows a merger of systems and cultures, which is manifested in a single, large organization, albeit geographically dispersed. The result is a combination of smaller regional organizations with a wide network of branches and facilities from which products and services are delivered.

Change has become the norm as banks attempt to assimilate new acquisitions into existing systems and cultures. For every acquisition that occurs, there is a conversion of systems to the primary bank data processing system for the reporting package, chart of accounts, and the ability to account for the new entity on a common basis. Beyond this, systems must merge so that all are operating on the same application system parameters. This is vital for a common product base and to ensure comparability to one another for evaluation. Another change occurs, procedural change, which is driven by the system change. This involves the flow of work and how it is performed. Finally, cultural change occurs. This is the most difficult to manage as well as to immediately identify. Cultural change is the change in business practice norms, attitudes, and beliefs that are unique to the organization. This change cannot occur overnight or even at the time the systems actually cutover. It will require months or years for the organizations to grow together and form a new culture.

All aspects of these organizational changes require the analysis, coordination, and tracking of some form or process leading to the culminating event of a cutover—physical combination of systems. Change is difficult and is a considerable challenge for virtually all business combinations. Combinations of this sort cannot effectively happen unless the process is well organized, a project is established, and the overall process is managed effectively. This requires specific methods for coordination of bank system conversion. System conversions typically involve mainframe applications, which are used by the bank to process the bulk of their products and services. However, system conversions today also include the various end user computing systems used by the bank. These include teller, platform automation systems, and other local area network systems not processed by the mainframe. Finally, telephone and voice systems must also be analyzed.

The purpose of this book is to outline the steps necessary for effective planning and coordination of bank system conversions: how they are organized, controlled, managed, monitored, and reported. The efficient and effective coordination of such conversions can save the organization tremendous amounts of time and money, which otherwise would be expended in cleanup, rework, and general catch up. Following the steps outlined will assist the reader in developing the standard functions necessary for systems conversions, which may not readily be available or for which costly outside consultants typically are employed.

Especially today, with major business combinations looming on the horizon, banks that have the ability to assimilate the acquired organization most quickly and efficiently will likely prevail and capture the greatest share of the market. Lessons can be learned from the stories told by large business combinations, such as NCR and AT&T, as well as other major combinations occurring outside the financial industry.

Developing templates and standard processes that can be used over and over for efficiently merging and converting banks is most important for any organization in an industry where growth and market share will occur through acquisition. In addition, companies other than banks are combining to capitalize on product lines or for strategic reasons such as expanded market areas, different product bases, and simply additional accounts or businesses.

In short, mergers and acquisitions are a fact of life in business and banking today. They will not likely go away, at least not in this country in the near term. It will be a decided advantage to any company to use the recommendations in this book to streamline and standardize the process which can facilitate the assimilation of mergers and acquisitions effectively.

## CHAPTER 1

Overview of System Conversion

OVERVIEW

Before one can begin to embark on the planning and implementation of a system conversion, a basic understanding of the nature of system conversions is a necessary foundation. This chapter acquaints the reader with the concept of system conversions and their applicability to the banking profession, their origin, as well as their scope and definition, all of vital importance today given the nature of mergers and acquisitions and the rapidity and frequency with which they occur.

The chapter provides the reader an understanding of and familiarity with

1. The history and origination of system conversion in the banking industry.
2. The definition and scope of system conversions in general, as well as the elements that constitute effective system conversions.
3. The rationale and purpose for conducting the bank conversion process, the necessity for controlling

the process within the organization and the benefits that result from following the steps and process in an organized manner, and the importance of the organization of the process to the future success of the bank.

4. The types of conversions that occur. This includes the culture necessary for effective bank conversions and an analysis of life beyond the systems standpoint, which predominantly drives the need for organized conversions. Finally the application of process steps in other areas requiring some element of conversion is also explored.

BACKGROUND

Usage in the Banking Industry

Within the banking industry, conversions have become practically routine functions or procedures for financial institutions, given the numbers of bank combinations that have occurred in the last two decades. With the change in bank branching laws, both national and state, many large financial institutions have embarked on a path of growth through acquisition and subsequent market share. To implement this strategy, the bank must have a well-seasoned staff and a set of procedures to ensure the effective conversion of bank systems as well as organizational and procedural conversions. In some cases, because the financial institution grows through acquisition, a separate department may be staffed to perform conversions, system or otherwise, on a regular basis. Service bureaus or large data centers typically will have staffs devoted to this discipline.

In either scenario, system conversions are an integral part of the successful combination of entities that will ultimately act as one. System conversions and their disciplines are not devoted solely to acquisitions and mergers. System conversions occur many times in the course of managing a business. Today, with the rapid growth and use of micro-computers and file servers and their considerable storage capability, many financial institutions rely on end-user computing for a wide variety of functions previously performed by the mainframe. As a result, whenever new software is introduced into the market or an upgrade is needed, some form of conversion will likely occur. Of course, in some cases, this conversion may be fully technical and transparent to the user department. However, for larger systems upon which greater reliance is placed, the transition from one software package to another may require the skills and steps outlined in this book.

Computer technology, particularly end-user computing technology, is growing at such a rapid pace that system conversions will be inevitable. Conversion disciplines will likely become a separate professional function, such as programming or the training required to become a computer technician. The point is that the process is needed and will not diminish in the foreseeable future. For the banking industry and other larger organizations that likely will be in acquisition modes and are very computer intensive, this may become a way of life.

Origination

Bank system conversions probably originated when financial institutions began to be computerized in the 1950s and 60s. At this time large mainframe computers were used to store and run the application systems used by banks for deposits, loans, and general ledger. In addition, large mainframe providers such as EDS began to evolve and flourish during this period. These providers had to learn firsthand how to convert organizations to their systems. In the early days the conversions were from manual systems to computerized systems rather than from one computer system to another, as is predominantly the case today.

During the 1970s and 80s, reliance on mainframe systems grew considerably for commercial banks. During this period computerization became a competitive necessity. Additionally, during this period, another phenomenon occurred that had major and widespread impact on the banking industry—deregulation. With deregulation, banks were forced to become more competitive with not only one another but with nonbanks offering financial services as well. Computerization played a major role in the competition. Less technical financial institutions were not able to keep pace with nonbanking institutions that were, in most cases, technically sophisticated. Because of this, technology became a major factor. To get products and services to market quickly, financial institutions had to rely on technology for development and implementation. As growth continued, federal and state laws began to relax allowing financial institutions to merge and/or acquire and own branches in different states. With banks branching this way, the door was opened for an increase in business combinations. As banks sought to be in particular communities and market areas, they could either build a branch or simply acquire one if consumer interest existed. Once this started to occur bank system conversions began to grow rather rapidly. Timely conversions that could be successfully accomplished with minimal slippage required the disciplines of system conversions.

SYSTEM CONVERSION DEFINED

Definition and Scope

System conversion is the process by which information is transferred from one method of processing to another, for the purpose of processing information in a combined manner. This transfer is made either from a manual operation to computers or from an existing software package and hardware to another software package or hardware. System conversions, in short, involve some form of transition of data.

The scope of system conversions is relatively broad, encompassing a multitude of tasks and areas. Don't let the title *system conversion* be misleading. Converting systems encompasses many operations leading to the combined processing activity that ultimately is the basis for providing services to customers. System conversions, therefore, involve actual procedures as well as policy decisions.

Following the conversion from one system to another, the new system may process information in a slightly different manner, which requires a decision to be made. Decisions of this nature usually involve policy decisions and must subsequently be brought to the attention of senior management. In addition, once the conversion occurs, procedural changes may result from the transition. This can involve the input of data to the major application systems or simply the preparation of information for input to the mainframe.

Communication is another aspect of system conversions. Changes in systems often result in different outputs to the bank's clients. When this happens, communicating with the customers is a necessity. In addition, internal users must be made aware of the changes in order to respond to customer inquiries, as well as for their own general knowledge.

All systems being converted must be subjected to compliance reviews to ensure that they meet the needs of the regulators and are not undisclosed. In short, the process of converting systems has a considerable scope involving a large number of people and departments.

Elements of a System Conversion

In its broadest form the system conversion process comprises four major areas:

1. Organization.
2. Preparation.
3. Data gathering.
4. Implementation.

Each of the four categories has a number of subcategories that compose the bulk of the tasks required during the conversion process. A fifth category involves nonsystem-related considerations, which is not a core category but nevertheless must be addressed. An expanded outline of these elements follows:

1. Organization.
    a. Identify the scope of the system conversion.
    b. Establish the authority to proceed, funding, and resources.
    c. Determine the system conversion coordinator.
    d. Identify the conversion committee.
    e. Establish subcommittees and charters.
    f. Develop the conversion plan and target the conversion date.
2. Process preparation.
    a. Prepare the conversion timeline and template.
    b. Prepare other project planning mechanisms.
    c. Prepare and conduct the kickoff meeting and agenda.
    d. Develop the meeting schedule, minutes, agenda format, and meeting flow.
    e. Provide executive summaries, communication mechanisms, and decisions.
    f. Prepare work papers and documentation.
    g. Assign responsibility to committee members and product leaders.
3. Data gathering.
    a. Site visits and floor plan development.
    b. Data gathering of application parameters/ settings and analysis of differences.
    c. Financial information comparisons and changes .
    d. Duplicate account number listing and analysis.
    e. Delivery and work flow.
    f. Forms gathering and analysis, internal/ external.

      g. System security (access) needs and planning.
      h. Courier schedules and workflow delivery and timing.
      i. Policy and procedures review.
      j. Third-party contracts/relationships.
      k. Location cutoffs and hours of operations.
4. Implementation.
      a. Technical installations and activations.
      b. Mainframe conversion process.
      c. Remote item processing activation.
      d. System security and user access to systems.
      e. Conversion weekend walkthrough planning.
      f. Conversion weekend activities/events.
      g. Conversion week activities.

The above steps complete the entire process of converting major systems for banks. Each of these elements will be explored in detail in subsequent chapters.

Although each conversion is different, the success of each depends upon adherence and attention to the steps broadly outlined. In some cases much more attention must be devoted to some areas and less to others. Areas such as work flow and delivery of work, however, will be critical elements in all circumstances and can make the difference between a successful and unsuccessful system conversion.

RATIONALE AND PURPOSE OF SYSTEM CONVERSIONS

The underlying reason for implementing the outlined steps, and for the system conversion process in general, is control and rapid return to normalcy. Although this may seem to be overly simplistic, one cannot grasp what is meant by return to normalcy without having gone through a system conversion that failed to return to normalcy. System conversions can take on a life of their own. The goal of any bank or other organization is to assimilate the new system or entity as fast as possible and return to business at hand. For financial institutions this is vital because of the customer impact, including the customers' confidence in their bank. System conversions that are not well planned and organized can strap the organization for months, making it virtually impossible to progress, to take advantage of new opportunities, or simply to conduct day-to-day business effectively.

Mention of system conversions having a life of their own refers to the pervasive nature of these processes. If the conversion results in out-of-balance conditions, or if work does not flow timely or effectively to the departments where the work is performed, the result can be major disruption, if not chaos. Unfortunately, banks cannot simply close their doors for a few days or weeks until things are back to normal. All efforts to correct situations gone awry must be made during regular hours and while new transactions continue to be made. This "moving target" can prolong the difficulties experienced for quite some time.

Rationale, therefore, for the systems conversion discipline is predominantly protection or insurance for the organization. Without it not only would the conversion go poorly, but it could conceivably erode the stature of the financial institution in the eyes of customers and the general public, thereby affecting the bank's status as a going concern. System conversions are thus a double-edged sword. On one hand they are necessary today in the acquisition and combination arena; on the other hand, conversions can greatly delay future plans or, in extreme cases, put an end to the bank's ability to grow at all.

Unfortunately, with the present level of computerization, no one can avoid system conversions, as complex as they may be, especially since there have been and will continue to be more business combinations than ever before.

A final word of caution to anyone about to embark on some form of combination or conversion: the bank cannot afford *not* to make the time, devote the resources, or focus on the elements necessary to make the system conversion as smooth as possible. The steps outlined in this book can increase odds for success and provide the financial institution with needed insurance for uninterrupted operations in the future.

TYPES OF CONVERSION

System conversions vary as to type. The most predominant, and the ones requiring the greatest degree of discipline and coordination, are mainframe system conversions. Mainframe system conversions fall into three categories:

1. Merger system conversion.
2. New acquisition conversion.
3. Change in data processor conversion.

In addition, the disciplines presented in this book can be used for smaller or less-pervasive events, which nevertheless require control and coordination. These events can fall into the following categories:

1. New software installation (conversion from old).
2. Software upgrades (new versions and releases).
3. New software installation/automation (conversion from manual to automated process).
4. Installation of new hardware.
5. Upgrade of existing hardware.

In all cases the steps and procedures outlined in this book, if used appropriately, will greatly enhance the possibility for timely and reasonably uneventful system conversions. For each a brief description and overview is provided.

Merger/System Conversion

Mergers represent the accounting combination of entities that either are part of the same parent or holding company or a totally new entity that has been purchased or otherwise acquired.

In the banking industry today mergers are normal occurrences. This is due, in some states, to the relaxing of state
laws affecting banking. Because of previous restrictions, organizations may have grown through acquisition but were
held as separate bank charters. In many ways this was inef-
ficient simply because individually chartered entities require
separate books and various other functions that are redun-
dantly performed.

Because banks, in most cases, can branch, parent companies have taken the opportunity to combine and eliminate
charters, while at the same time eliminating redundant duties. To accomplish this, a fairly sizable system conversion
must occur, consisting of combining general ledgers, loans,
and deposits to name a few. Depending on how much free-
dom the previous charter permitted, this may or may not be
intensive.

Bank mergers always require a mainframe system conversion (merger); the only issue regarding mergers is that in
most cases the entities could be on the same system, thus
requiring a merging of parameters and other programs. Although this may sound relatively simple, it should never be
taken lightly. Regardless of whether the entities are on the
same system, parameter settings and other advances may
exist that will require great care in the combination.

New Acquisition Conversion

In contrast to mergers, new acquisitions are almost always a
combination of two completely different systems. This is by
far the most complex system conversion because not only is it
a conversion of two separate systems and organizations, but
two completely different systems. In this scenario, once it is
established what parameters are to be used or what products
and services will be offered, the conversion methodology for
combining data from different systems must be completed.
This requires much discussion and analysis of both systems
by the programming staffs of each data processor.

In this scenario, two changes are occurring at once: the systems and also the procedures, policies, products, and services of two different entities. As a result the time frame required for this type of conversion is more lengthy than that of the merger.

Change in Data Processor Conversion

The last of the mainframe conversions is less complex than the previous one but nevertheless a challenge. In this case the bank is changing from one data processor to another. This almost always involves a complete change in all major software used by the financial institution. The change includes the core systems such as deposits, loans, and financial control. This type of conversion requires a similar skill set, but is direct in that one software system is being replaced by another.

This will certainly require a change in user display screens, procedures, and the like due to the different software now in use, and will likely impact the customer. Customers of the bank may experience a different ATM display which may cause concern requiring communication.

New Software Installation (Conversion from Old)

Software transitions can be very demanding depending on what the software is expected to do. This can be a specific mainframe software program such as deposits, or it may be microcomputer-based, such as a conversion from WordPerfect wordprocessing software to Microsoft Word. In either case the transition is much narrower than was defined in the overall mainframe conversion scenarios. Again, regardless of the software change occurring, the disciplines must be included to ensure that no data is lost or carried over improperly.

Software changes will occur with some frequency, particularly in the end-user computing world. With changes

occurring as rapidly as they are, new options become available daily. This presents significant challenges to the Information System Division, particularly if there is a large base
of equipment involved.

Software Upgrades
(New Versions and Releases)

Similar to software changes, upgrades will require a change
to the existing software currently used. This again, can apply in either the mainframe or end user computing worlds.
When upgrades or new releases are developed, the bank
must ensure that the upgraded software carries over the
data previously stored. This requires coordination, timing,
and care. An upgrade demands the conversion skills necessary for any of the previous situations, only with less intensity and depth.

New Software Installation/Automation
(Conversion from Manual to
Automated Processes)

The use of completely new software to replace or enhance a
manual system requires different skills from the other types
of conversion. Whenever manual processes are to be replaced by automated systems, the manual flow should be
mapped using flowcharts. This may facilitate designing or
customizing the new software. In this scenario data flow
diagrams are very useful, as in the Systems Development
Life Cycle (SDLC) approach.

Unlike the others, this conversion is unique. There is no
programming migration to occur, only new processing on an
automated system. If the new software is designed properly
or purchased effectively to meet the need, the transition
process can be relatively simple. However, if difficulty occurs because of lack of planning and coordination, trust will
erode and users will likely continue to rely on manual sys-

tems either to verify the accuracy of the automated systems or to perform the work, both of which are unacceptable. These unique concerns must not be treated lightly, because they may be the cause of many failures and wasted costs on unnecessary software.

Installation of New Hardware

One cannot omit hardware when talking of conversions. As with software, hardware must be coordinated effectively to ensure a smooth transition and adequate usage. A new printer, file server, or central processing unit (CPU) of a computer can greatly improve overall productivity if properly implemented. Although extensive programming may not be demanded as fully as with software conversions, the steps clearly must be followed to transition of a new piece of equipment. Hardware conversions generally are costly and, therefore, are usually fully justified and analyzed in advance. Unfortunately, this is where further critical analysis typically stops. The installation of new hardware not only requires testing but training and understanding as well. This will go a long way in making the process smooth. Without attention to these elements the hardware will not be adequately utilized and will not provide the organization with the type of return it may have originally projected in the purchase analysis. New hardware installations can include not only file servers, but also equipment such as new telephone systems (PBXs), networks, routers, and microcomputers.

Upgrade of Existing Hardware

Although similar to the installation of new hardware, upgrading existing hardware requires transition from an older model to a newer, more advanced model. This transition can be very complex, because it is seldom plug and play. In most cases upgrading hardware requires the same disciplines and utilization found in the proposed conversion methodology because any new or upgraded hardware has different elements or improvements to it. This demands additional testing and training.

OTHER USES OF THE CONVERSION METHODOLOGY

As you will see, the overall steps and discipline suggested for the conversion process can be applied in other circumstances. To some degree the approach used is transferable to other areas when attempting to implement or change an existing procedure, whether manual or automatic. The tasks outlined follow a logical sequence and are designed to function as a template that can be used in many different processes to ensure successful transitions. To that end the approach outlined in this book should not be viewed narrowly. It can be broadly applied to a wide variety of disciplines.

In many ways the conversion methodology follows a project management methodology but defines the major categories and standard tasks that should be considered in any conversion, whether mainframe, end user, or simply a process requiring these steps. The template approach will force consideration of tasks and issues which may not readily come to mind in the process. The net result will be effective and timely conversions.

CULTURE

The chapter cannot be considered complete without a discussion of organizational culture. Some organizations do not have a culture for any type of transition or conversion; others do. Building a culture conducive to this type of discipline emphasizes the way bank managers think. In other words, whenever a conversion is required as a result of an acquisition, merger, or upgrade of software, the standard approach is to begin the process outlined in this book. No decision needs to be made; it is a natural occurrence. This is the ideal.

When bank managers operate this way, everyone is planning by the same rules and the conversion begins. There is no time wasted in procrastination, or decision making that may be nonproductive or delay the timing of the conversion. The process is simply undertaken, as second nature, using the conversion methodology steps. When this mentality is present in the financial institution, a culture for effective conversions has been achieved.

Culture generally refers to the norms and practices accepted by a society or group of people representing their collective thoughts and beliefs. When a culture has been established, the process becomes the norm, and is simply used whenever a situation arises.

Another aspect of the development of a culture is the concept of change. Conversions are changes. As such any conversion has the capability of affecting the organization by altering procedures and transitioning to some unknown process, software, or procedure. This can be of tremendous concern to employees and management alike. Change keeps people on edge; the element of the unknown causes employees sometimes to react in nonproductive, nonanticipated, or nondesired ways. If a bank or other organization has remained relatively stable and unchanged for a period of time, when a transition does occur it can be a major upheaval. This upheaval manifests itself in incorrect handling, improper procedure utilization, and general disruption. Culturally, this may be so much of a shock to the organization that it either cannot recover or may require considerable time for complete healing and recovery, both of which are unacceptable.

The 1990s have proven to be a decade of change. Technology keeps moving with new software and upgrades literally emerging every day. Today more than ever before decisions must be made about basic processing. It often happens that when an organization becomes completely comfortable with a piece of software, major system, or hardware, the system is replaced by an upgraded version and support ceases. This is a normal occurrence today.

Unfortunately, now it is not the bank that drives the need for change but rather the vendor, or competitor who is converting to the new product. The reason for this is that the new products invariably are better and more functional, creating more potential value. Not converting can cause a bank to remain out of step with the industry. The problem is that software and hardware development is progressing at an accelerated rate, and the static environments of the past simply will not do. An educator and futurist, Dr. Leo Coleman, commented in a recent talk that the knowledge base is now doubling every three years for high technology, but for super-high technology knowledge is doubling every year. As a result of this phenomenon, it is little wonder that new hardware and software appear on the market seemingly every year. This fast pace is catching some banks on their heels and keeping them there. In other words, high technology is going to keep changing; banks can survive only by their ability to cope and keep up with the changes. To keep up it will be necessary to change bank cultures to ones of learning. The concept of the learning organization is not new, but it has been evolving because of these changes. Banks must teach employees to learn to learn, as is now being done in the college environment.

Without a culture that promotes change and adaptability to new technologies, the organization will remain brittle and will likely break when the change becomes too great. This will cause the demise of the organization, as is already the case with many banks in the United States. For this reason the concept of system conversions, which may appear to be more of a procedural narrative on the surface, actually is much more. The process is a road map to permit the organization to cope with change, to not be caught on its heels but rather its toes, ready to embrace change and capable of assimilating any transition. The establishment of this type of culture must emanate from senior management and requires much more than merely authoring a directive. Employees and managers must be shown the way. Neither the subdivision phenomenon (houses going up overnight) nor the mass production of automobiles could have occurred unless a blueprint for standard procedures and processes for building these products had first been developed. In banks, especially today, this blueprint has to be the conversion methodology that is discussed in detail in this book. A conversion blueprint will empower the organization to act quickly and efficiently in a common way when confronted with the need for change. It is a defined and proven methodology that will supply the bank with the appropriate tools for success.

Once this culture is established, new opportunities will abound for the organization. Opportunities previously left to others may now be considered more often, and this can change a bank into a proactive player in the marketplace rather than a reactive entity waiting for change to be imposed. The development of this culture is critical today. Technology is not going to slow or stop. New opportunities will arise daily. Each will challenge us to consider the opportunities and how they apply to us and our customers. In short, critical analysis will be a norm in everyday work. Together with critical analysis come learning and knowledge, which must be ongoing, never ceasing. These are the marching orders for banking and other professions for the rest of this decade and beyond. Those able to understand and grasp this concept will survive, those who do not, will not survive—it is as simple as that.

At the start of this century Frederick Winslow Taylor developed what he called the *Principles of Scientific Management*. He recognized, at the time, that the world was changing and that organizations needed methodologies for dealing with change and to gain efficiencies that would not only help them cope with the changes occurring but also to prepare them for the new order.

The change that was occurring was industrialization. Managers were ill prepared to deal with the dynamics of factories and manufacturing entities, the massive number of workers, and new machinery. Frederick Taylor's principles helped to cut through the veil of uncertainty and enabled organizations to grow into the giants they are today. We, in the latter part of the same century, are going through a similar change. The only difference is that now information, not industrialization, is driving this change. We as bankers, and managers, need the tools and processes that will help us to cut through another veil of uncertainty, to allow us to be propelled into the information world and build new giants. The principles of conversion management can go a long way toward providing the bank with the tools necessary for this transition. For this reason the following chapters outline the steps and details that will help banks to establish this culture.

SUMMARY

System conversion for banks has a decided procedural or tactical ring to it. This chapter has attempted to lay the groundwork for the rationale as well as present a brief history and definition of what is meant by bank systems conversion management. The goal of the chapter is to establish that this process is not merely a "how to" procedure, but one that has much broader implications. In this sense, justification, rationale, and even the dynamics of the establishment of a culture for change are outlined. Conversions are phenomena that are not altogether new but that are now occurring with increasing frequency—so much so that the discipline itself is growing in importance and stature. It should become, in the author's opinion, a defined function unto itself, as in system programming or systems analysis. Conversions will permeate the industry in the years to come because of the rapid growth of technology and growing number of business combinations already occurring. In short, conversions will not go away, they will increase in number and frequency, becoming a routine occurrence.

As banking organizations plan to be competitors or growing concerns in the marketplace, the skills and methodology required in system conversions will be mandatory. The bank must be positioned to change and be able to embrace change. This is not simply stated in words, or in a mission statement; the bank must have a tangible methodology for effecting change, otherwise it will not occur. The blueprint for transition must be established, used, and practiced to enable the financial institution to evolve or develop a culture for change that will allow the entity to move quickly and efficiently when opportunities arise. The success of a business combination does not result from the awarding of the winning bid. Success comes from smooth assimilation of the two organizations both culturally and in systems conversion. Only in this way can the bank grow effectively for the future and take advantage of change with confidence.

Organization of the System Conversion

OVERVIEW

Planning and organizing the system conversion process require care and attention. Much of the success of the overall conversion depends on how well it is organized. Chapter 2 outlines and defines the steps required to organize the system conversion process and explains how to develop the structure from which tasks will be completed. The goal of this segment is to provide legitimacy and commitment to the system conversion, to have management, from the top down, commit the resources necessary to organize the conversion into a defined structure.

After studying Chapter 2 the reader will

1. Be able to identify and define the scope/boundaries of the conversion to be undertaken. (This will enable the reader to understand what is and what is not included in the process.)
2. Understand how to go about establishing the authority to proceed, funding and obtaining the

resources necessary for beginning to coordinate the entire conversion process.

3. Understand the skills necessary for selecting the conversion coordinator and how to proceed with the identification of the conversion coordinator.

4. Understand the importance and purpose of the conversion committee, how to go about its selection, and develop the skills necessary for conversion committee participants.

5. Understand the purpose and role of subcommittees as well as their composition, the skills required of subcommittee members, and the selection process.

6. Develop an understanding of the necessity of a conversion plan, how to prepare a conversion plan, and how to target the conversion or cutover date.

System conversions are seldom processes that can begin overnight. They require time for planning and preparation. The success of the system conversion depends on a well thought out plan and proper organization of the process. For this reason great care and attention should be focused on the elements in this chapter as a prerequisite for successful conversions.

Fortunately organization and preparation of the system conversion does not require a lot of time, as the bank may not have months to plan or prepare and still take advantage of an opportunity. What is required, however, is a commitment to the organization and a focus on the meaning of the elements.

IDENTIFY THE SCOPE OF THE SYSTEM CONVERSION

In the first chapter the author spoke of several types of system conversions. These were the basic system conversion categories into which most system conversions will fall.

Typically, the need for a system conversion results from the type of transition to be undertaken. This is first determined after the president, board of directors, or other decision-making authorities announce the planned transition. Once this is determined, it is relatively simple to ascertain the type of system conversion needed. A system conversion can take many forms. It does not have to be a computer system, but can be a manual system. However, the odds of a computer application being involved are quite great. For this reason, the focus of this book is computer-related system conversions. In all cases, however, the reader must assume that any transition requires some form of system conversion.

If the financial institution has announced a combination in the form of an acquisition or merger, a mainframe system conversion will always be necessary. A change in mainframe data processor will also require a major system conversion. Purchase of a new software product (application system) will require some form of system conversion, but it will not be as extensive as with a mainframe conversion.

Upon notification of the type of business transition that will occur, management or the coordinator of the impending transition should immediately define the scope of the transition—what it is and what it is not.

This is important because organizing an effective conversion is difficult unless some boundaries are established. In addition, since a business combination or transition is terminal, that is it will end, boundaries are needed to determine at what point it will end. In this way subsequent operations can be planned or, at least, an understanding can be gained of what other major issues are around the corner to allow ample time for assimilation. Depending on the nature of the transition or combination, it should be understood that a period of adjustment or simply settling down will occur. This must happen whether or not the bank wants it. If it is not planned for in the process, other events may be occurring during this period that will cause confusion and concern. As the bank is transitioning, taking on additional major projects or events can unduly tax the staff and cause technical difficulties. For this reason the period of adjustment must be built into the conversion timeline just as any other task would be.

Establishing the boundaries for the conversion provides greater precision and understanding of how long resources will be committed and when normalcy will again be attained. Taking time to establish the scope helps to clarify what aspects of the system conversion will or will not be considered. Once a system conversion process begins, a definite tendency exists to uncover other areas of opportunity or need. The defined transition period cannot achieve everything and cure all of the bank's ills. If transition goals are not clearly defined, resources may be diverted to other tangential areas that may not focus on the main objective. This, by far, creates the greatest opportunity for slippage, delaying the overall conversion beyond the time frame originally anticipated. If the bank wishes to make other changes during the conversion period (it may be appropriate to do so), the additional areas must clearly be identified and planned for.

A word of caution! When defining the scope of a particular bank transition, keep in mind the main objective of the transition in its simplest form and focus all resources and funds toward the main objective. Taking on subsidiary projects or within conversions is extremely risky for even the most seasoned system conversion coordinator. If the goal of the business transition is to convert an acquired bank to the mainframe system of the acquiring bank, then focus only on this. Avoid changing other software not directly related or unnecessary to the conversion process, as this adds another element of risk that will likely contribute to the overall detriment of the conversion.

It is strongly recommended that the goals and objectives, or at least the outcomes, of the conversion process be very clearly defined before the process actually begins. This will go a long way toward providing legitimacy, support and organization to the conversion at the outset.

AUTHORIZATION TO PROCEED, FUNDING, AND RESOURCES

All projects whether large or small cost money and time and therefore will likely require approval or authorization to proceed. When the decision has been made to proceed with the business transition, regardless of its nature, a primary owner or champion must emerge. This typically will be the initiator of the business transition, and will likely be a professional at the upper levels in the organization, a decision maker. This individual will not coordinate the system conversion on a day-to-day basis but will provide the initial authority and impetus to proceed. System conversions regarding bank acquisitions, mergers, or change in data processor require a considerable commitment. As such the initiator must clearly articulate the resource and funding requirements to the bank president and/or board of directors. It is extremely important, if not vital, to obtain the full commitment and support of the top executive officer in the bank because the resource commitment will cross many boundaries, affecting many departments and managers. These managers may or may not be involved in the process, but must absolutely be supportive of the process and the time required on the part of their own departmental resources. Politically, once the president and/or CEO has embraced the system conversion and will support the process, he or she can influence other interdisciplinary managers to ensure that they provide the type of support necessary to make the conversion successful. This requires a commitment to prioritize ordinary daily duties or conversion-related work. If both are considered a priority and managers place little emphasis on the system conversion, even though their staff may have tasks to perform in the conversion, staff members will always focus on departmental duties first. This is obviously detrimental to the system conversion and will most likely delay it.

System conversions that are organization-wide require an overall understanding that a timely and effective conversion is the priority so that focus can be properly directed. To attain this, top down support is an absolute must. If this is not clearly communicated to the managers of the bank, support will not be forthcoming, and the bank is in for a protracted conversion. Remember, some of the resources involved in the system conversion will be the employees of a number of different managers throughout the bank. System conversions seldom can be outsourced because success requires existing knowledge and how systems will ultimately be changed or effectively combined. To do this, existing bank knowledge must be utilized, which originates from employees and managers.

Funding is also a major consideration. It must be clear from the outset, that some work will not be performed or must be postponed due to the priority of the system conversion. This can have a monetary impact on the bank and therefore must be known up front, so as to avoid surprises. If this is unacceptable, then it is necessary to back-fill key employees involved in the system conversion with others or even outside temporary services. In other words, commitment of employee time should be quantified to the extent possible and communicated to the managers. An estimate of the impact of their conversion involvement should occur to determine whether this is acceptable or not. In addition, a budget should be established for the system conversion, beyond the costs of the business transaction. This may involve outsourced assistance, additional reporting, communications, or simply the cost of preventing the day-to-day work from being performed.

Once the conversion coordinator is selected, it is extremely likely that he or she will be fully committed to the process for two to six or more months, depending on the type and size of the system conversion. If this individual is currently performing an important function that is a prerequisite for coordinating the conversion effort, a void will be created that will need to be filled.

Finally, it is of utmost importance that a sponsor be named as overall champion of the conversion project. As stated previously, this should be either the president or a member of senior management who also is a decision maker. The sponsor initiates the overall conversion project and puts it into motion. It is to this individual that the system conversion coordinator will report directly. The role of the sponsor is to ensure that the funding and resources are properly committed to the process and to report to the president or board of directors when issues arise. The position of sponsor must not be deemphasized. Effective system conversion projects of wide scope have a much greater likelihood of success with an active sponsor. The sponsor, however, need not be involved in the day-to-day process of conversion, as this is the role of the conversion coordinator. But the sponsor must be advised regularly as to the project status to keep others within the bank informed and focused. Again, major system conversions are pervasive, that is, they affect virtually all aspects of the bank. An effective sponsor ensures that key executives are regularly informed of the progress and issues. Issues include the need for additional funding, additional resources, or other elements to ensure the success of the process. Finally, the sponsor adds a top down commitment and understanding of the effort and workload involved in the system conversion process.

DETERMINE THE SYSTEM CONVERSION COORDINATOR

The system conversion coordinator is the most important role in the overall conversion process, second only to the system conversion sponsor. The system conversion coordinator is the individual who coordinates the day-to-day activities of the conversion. The conversion sponsor usually selects the system conversion coordinator. The conversion coordinator should come from the bank itself, although the position can be outsourced. The benefit of internal selection is that the employee knows the organization, the people, and the procedures. This can go a long way toward making the process successful and is a decided asset. Selection of the conversion coordinator is an important decision. This decision involves four steps:

1. Define the job, its responsibilities and tasks.
2. Identify the skills and characteristics needed.
3. Identify the position in the organization required for effective coordinator.
4. Identify candidates and make the selection.

Define the Job, Responsibilities, and Tasks

The conversion sponsor should formally draft a job description and list of responsibilities for the system conversion coordinator. Much like defining the scope of the conversion, a written job description establishes boundaries identifying what the job is and is not. A clear understanding of the nature and responsibilities of the job are needed to select the proper coordinator. The job description can be used again in the future for other system conversion activities or projects. Actually, it could become the job description for a permanent system conversion coordinator if the bank is likely to be involved in numerous conversions in the future. This is not altogether far fetched today. Because of the reliance on systems, and the various types of conversions discussed in Chapter 1, some form of system conversion will be occurring, with frequency, in the years to come.

Responsibilities of the system conversion coordinator include

- Selection of conversion committee members.
- Coordination and facilitation of regular (weekly or every other week) conversion committee meetings.
- Development of the system conversion project plan.

- Development of the system conversion timeline.
- Determination and organization of critical tasks, including determining person hours for completion and estimation of completion targets.
- Maintaining system conversion documentation, including meeting minutes and project plan and timeline updates.
- Development and submission of regular summary reports to the conversion sponsor and senior management.
- Monitoring and ensuring the completion of committee member tasks in accordance with stated time frames.
- Matrix management of committee members and other parties to the system conversion process.
- Performance of conversion tasks as defined.
- Liaison with third-party vendors and point of escalation to third-party senior management as required during the process.
- Overall mediator and facilitator of the process.

A sound understanding of the basic job description permits the conversion sponsor to select the appropriate individual for the position.

Identification of Skills and Characteristics

Once the basic job description has been developed, the next major step is to understand the type of individual needed to carry out such duties. In order to make an effective selection, the conversion sponsor should seek an individual that possesses the following skills and characteristics:

1. Skills:
   a. Project management experience and abilities.
   b. Management experience, both mid-level and supervisory type background (minimum of three years).

   c. Strong facilitation skills for coordinating
      effective meetings and for distributing work
      and responsibilities.
   d. Matrix management experience.
   e. Strong time management skills.
   f. Broad bank experience and background
      (experience in a number of areas).
2. Characteristics:
   a. Recognized/respected individual in the
      organization.
   b. Positive bankwide reputation for getting things
      done.
   c. Apolitical—ability to cross numerous
      boundaries without being perceived as
      fulfilling his or her own agenda.
   d. Trusted individual, one whom people feel
      comfortable confiding in.
   e. Intense sense of urgency and commitment;
      recognizes importance of a target deadline and
      accepts this as the primary directive.

Characteristics are extremely important in ensuring that the
process actually will be completed. In this sense two characteristic are of special importance, (1) apolitical nature and (2)
sense of urgency and time. In the selection of a coordinator,
these are of vital importance to guarantee success. Political
individuals normally are perceived as such and cause wari-
ness on the part of people with whom they work. This
characteristic cannot be tolerated in a system conversion
process. The ability to cross numerous boundaries without
causing fear in people who interface with the system conversion coordinator allows individuals to be more open and
communicate concerns vital to a system conversion process.
Especially in times of change, when staff employees are most
wary, it is important that the coordinator be perceived as
nonthreatening and trustworthy. In this way people will be

willing to work with the coordinator to achieve the goals of the conversion.

Another vital characteristic is a sense of urgency. When selecting the conversion coordinator, care must be taken to find an individual who understands urgency. This is a characteristic of people who have a talent for getting things done within allotted time frames. A major system conversion must be accomplished within very definite, specified time frames in order for the bank to plan accurately and get back to normalcy. The speed and predictability of the system conversion process are what allows the organization to capitalize on opportunities, both now and in the future. System conversions that continually slip or are indefinitely delayed will not instill confidence and will cause the bank to forfeit opportunities and lose confidence for the future. The system conversion coordinator must possess this sense of urgency, with the ability to achieve the stated conversion date. An individual with this characteristic, coupled with the project management skills, will ensure that the right tasks are completed at the right times. This is truly a management venture and must be managed carefully. Conversions of this nature do not occur by themselves but must be carefully controlled, shepherded, and moved toward a definite cutover. An inadequate coordinator may not have the skills to accomplish routines necessary to carefully complete the most mundane of tasks on a timely basis, or at least to know why one was not completed. The proper type of disposition will ensure greater success for the future.

Finally, the addition of broad bank experience is a decided plus. When the system conversion coordinator is conversant with terminology and operations of the bank, greater confidence arises simply because the language and issues are understood. This will greatly assist the conversion coordinator in anticipating where problems may occur or recognizing areas where greater clarification is required.

Position Held within the Organization

The system conversion coordinator need not be a member of senior management to be effective. However, it is important that the individual selected be a seasoned manager, typically at the middle management level. The main reason for this is that the coordinator will be managing a number of people at peer level, below, and in some cases above as well. A solid middle manager position supplies the right level of credibility and lends confidence to the overall committee to proceed.

The conversion coordinator reports directly to the overall conversion sponsor who typically is a senior manager, if not the president. The coordinator must be able to relate well to the CEO and other senior managers in presenting reports, status, and updates, and in fielding questions, comments, and concerns that arise during the process. For these reasons it is necessary that the coordinator be of proper rank in the organization, and be perceived so by other managers and parties to the process. In many ways the system conversion coordinator must rely on his or her reputation and abilities to accomplish the tasks required in the project plan.

Identify Candidates and Make the Selection

The skills and characteristics outlined previously should be used as a template for the selection of the system conversion coordinator. The bank may not be able to identify someone with all of the characteristics and skills. However, compared to other candidates, the coordinator will be the one with the edge in the majority of the areas. It is important that the selected individual have a broad range of characteristics and skills rather than being more expert in fewer areas.

The selection process should evaluate a list of individuals perceived to have the skills and characteristics previously identified. One way to do this is to have senior managers advance names for consideration based upon defined criteria (characteristics and skills). The conversion sponsor should actually interview and evaluate the candidates advanced for consideration. Interviews help to legitimize the process and demonstrate the importance of the overall system conversion. Furthermore, they help the conversion sponsor to gain an understanding of what the candidate can and cannot do.

CHOOSING THE CONVERSION COMMITTEE

Once the system conversion coordinator is selected, his or her first task will be to organize the conversion committee. The conversion committee is the group empowered to perform the system conversion tasks and duties. This group is made up of staff members representing the major disciplines involved in the system conversion. In most cases a typical system conversion committee consists of the following core disciplines:

1. System programmer(s).
2. Audit representative.
3. Operational managers.
4. Marketing/communication representative.
5. Compliance representative.
6. Information systems representative.
7. Sales representative.
8. Training representative.

Each of the above are broad categories, representing functional areas. This core group should remain the same for virtually all system conversions. The only area that typically changes in composition and number is operational managers. Each category is defined in detail below.

System Programmers

System programmers are most typically involved when a major mainframe system conversion occurs, however they could be involved even in situations regarding microcom-

puter or minicomputer conversions. The system programmer or analyst is vital to the process, regardless if the bank
utilizes a service bureau or has an in-house mainframe.
System programmers map, analyze, and actually perform
the programming that will merge the two systems or set up
the parameters for a conversion from a manual procedure to
an electronic system. As such they must be represented on
the committee to lend structure to the discussion, and guide
operational users as to what can and cannot be done. System
programmers lay out the plan for the necessary programming to effect the conversion.

System programmers and/or analysts must be involved in the system conversion from start to finish. When
the actual conversion occurs, there will be several weeks in
which close scrutiny of how the combined system operates
must occur to ensure that interest is being calculated as
disclosed, statements generated when required, and the
myriad of other parameters and programs are operating
correctly. System programmers report directly either to the
information systems division of the bank or to the service
bureau if data processing is outsourced. During the system
conversion process, however, and in conjunction with the
conversion committee, the system programmer must report
directly to the system conversion coordinator on a matrix
basis.

Audit Representative

The audit representative is an important position on the
system conversion committee. Auditors are trained to be
professionally skeptical. As a result of this propensity, they
can be instrumental in uncovering details in the system
conversion process that may go unnoticed by others. Once
the conversion occurs, auditors will ultimately be auditing
the systems in their normal audit programs. Because of this,
to the extent they can participate and shed light on areas of
concern prior to actual programming time, future problems

may be avoided. The audit representative should not set policy or establish procedures relative to the system conversion but certainly can review processes and other setups to ensure that pitfalls likely to be a problem in the future are uncovered. As such, the role of the audit representative is more observer or critic rather than direct participant. Their function is to comment on and critically review programs and other processes established during the system conversion to ensure proper handling. The audit representative will be directed by the system conversion coordinator on a matrix basis to assess particular areas that may be more sensitive than others.

Operational Managers

Operational managers will vary by the type of system conversion. These individuals represent the true users of the systems and must be major players in the overall process. Operational managers, in a mainframe system conversion, will include those departments and functional areas that interact with the systems. These include

1. Deposit operations.
2. Loan operations.
3. Remote (check) processing.
4. Bookkeeping and statement preparation.
5. General ledger (accounting).
6. ATMs.
7. Customer service.
8. Cash management.
9. Credit/collections.

Either the manager or a key representative of each of the above areas must be represented on the system conversion committee. The selection of the individuals should be made between the system conversion coordinator and the manager of each of the operational departments. As previously stated, the ultimate representative may be the manager of the area, if that is the appropriate individual. In other cases the manager of the department will know who, in that area, is the strongest individual to represent the needs of the operational area most effectively. In either case, selection should be made in conjunction with the manager. The system conversion coordinator should avoid making the decision alone and contacting directly the desired individual. This would be inappropriate and could cause problems between the system conversion coordinator and the managers of the operational area.

It must also be remembered that the operational areas still have a day-to-day job to do. Therefore the system conversion coordinator should be sensitive to the fact that whoever is involved will still be required to perform daily functions as well and will be accountable to their manager for executing these duties. Sensitivity to this fact, and proper initial communication with the manager of the operational area, will greatly facilitate the selection process while maintaining rapport.

In other types of system conversions, all of the operational departments do not need to be represented as they do in mainframe system conversion. If the system conversion is an upgrade or other end-user type conversion, different or more selected departments may be required. Selection of the operational departments to be represented is the job of the system conversion coordinator, based upon the nature of the system being added, upgraded, or converted.

Marketing/Communication Representative

If the conversion is a merger or acquisition, the impact on the organization is pervasive. Because of this, there will be a marketing or customer communication impact. This may involve the change of customer disclosures, brochures, or other product communications, including service charge brochures. All of these will require some form of analysis to make changes. The marketing and communication representative is responsible for pulling together all aspects of customer communications and advertising that should be involved in the overall conversion. In addition to product information, a number of other communication devices will require analysis. These include customer notices, statements, deposit slips, receipts, passbooks, notes, applications, loan documentation, and other types of printed material. Because of the volume of printed material, involvement of the marketing/communication officer is a must for any system conversion.

In addition to printed material, other forms of communication will likely be affected during the process. These include signage, radio and television advertisements, and billboard advertising. Customer signs within the lobby will also be a part of the concern of this individual. The marketing/communication representative, therefore, is a vital member of the system conversion for most, if not all, system conversions.

Compliance Representative

The compliance representative is becoming a more important addition to the system conversion committee. Compliance must review literally all communications to ensure that they adhere to all bank regulations and protect the bank from improper communications and/or disclosures. In addition to printed matter, compliance representatives must also review how the programs are being set up to ensure that they match what is being told to customers, both in correspondence and in advertisements. It is a very important responsibility of the committee to ensure that the bank communicates properly to customers to avoid a negative impact on customer relations. Furthermore, the bank will continue to be examined. Care taken during the conversion process will aid greatly in avoiding problems that may be uncovered later during a bank examination.

Information Systems Representative

In all circumstances, an information systems representative should be a part of the committee. For most conversions the functions represented by information systems will be affected. These will likely include network and data communications, end-user computing, telecommunications, and other areas. A major part of this responsibility is how products and services are delivered to the customer. Information systems typically has much to do with this. Areas potentially affected involve services such as interactive voice response systems (IVR), home banking (if applicable), ATM connectivity, and the delivery of communications, both voice and data to the bank users, many of whom can change during the system conversion process. The information systems representative should be the individual best suited to represent all aspects of information systems.

Sales Representative

The sales representative is included to articulate the needs of the sales areas during the process, particularly when changes are being made that will affect customers. The sales representative should be a retail as well as a commercial representative, although the most important would likely be the retail platform area. The sales representative provides input to the changes being made from a sales standpoint, because most system conversions are typically performed by operational representatives. Operations people do not always consider all aspects or needs of the sales areas when changes are made. For this reason the addition of sales helps to bring out an additional perspective when issues are brought to the committee for discussion. Many system conversion committees have not included sales. However, because of the intensity of sales in the banking industry and the impact on customers, the inclusion of sales representatives is strongly recommended.

Training Representative

Training is an extremely important part of any system conversion. By definition, a system conversion denotes change. Whenever change occurs, new procedures will be developed, new systems added, and in general a change takes place in the way staff personnel perform. When this happens, training is a necessity to ensure that the staff is current with the changes and prepared to make such changes as efficiently as possible. Consequently, another major player on the committee is the training manager, or someone who can represent the needs of the staff at large and to plan and organize required training.

Training almost always occurs with any type of system conversion. This training must be planned, with arrangements made for logistics and implementation prior to the changes taking effect. This involves much planning and scheduling, and therefore requires someone who can take responsibility for this type of discipline. If the bank does not have a separate training department, the system conversion coordinator must recommend an individual who has an understanding of the training needs that will likely be required. This could be a member of human resources or it could simply be an individual who has conducted a substantial portion of the training for the bank. Additionally, the training function could be represented by an outside consultant or representative from the service bureau if the bank outsources its data processing. In any event the representation is an absolute must. Not considering training needs could be extremely detrimental to the system conversion once cutover occurs.

Care should be taken in identifying and selecting system conversion committee members. They are the individuals who will actually perform or coordinate the voluminous tasks that must be accomplished during major system conversions. Most conversions require so much effort and work that it is virtually impossible for a small team to be expected to accomplish it smoothly. The conversion committee, if structured as recommended, will ensure that all key disciplines involved in the conversion are represented. Each member of the committee is responsible for coordinating his or her own group or subcommittee for the execution of tasks and duties, as discussed in the next section.

ESTABLISHING SUBCOMMITTEES AND CHARTERS

Once the overall system conversion committee composition has been completed, subcommittees need to be formed. Each discipline represented on the overall system conversion committee will, in most cases, need to establish a subcommittee for the execution of the tasks that will be identified on the project plan. The representative on the system conversion committee will chair the subcommittee and is responsible not only for identifying individuals who will participate in the subcommittee meeting but will also facilitate the subcommittee meetings and report progress to the system conversion committee. Often the individual representing the discipline on the system conversion committee is the manager of the area represented. If this is the case, their subcommittee will likely be their own staff. In this case subcommittee meetings can occur as part of the normal series of departmental meetings.

Subcommittees, like the overall system conversion committee, must be organized and structured. This means they must develop a form of mission or charter that identifies their purpose and sets in motion what is expected. Remember the subcommittee, also, is terminal in that it will disband after the system conversion timeline is completely satisfied. The orders for the subcommittee will be contained in the overall conversion plan, which is developed by the system conversion coordinator.

The system conversion committee member will function similarly to the system conversion coordinator. In that respect this individual is responsible for coordinating and facilitating subcommittee meetings. In addition this committee person will be accountable for the completion of all tasks on the conversion plan (through other subcommittee members) and will report regular progress at the system conversion meeting. In other words, the subcommittee is actually where the actual work will be performed for all aspects of the system conversion. To that end it must be staffed with individuals who not only are knowledgeable about the tasks required, but staff employees who will have the time and sense of urgency to accomplish these tasks. The latter requirement, time, may be more difficult because the subcommittee members also have full-time jobs to perform on a regular basis. As a result, the facilitation of the work performed by this group becomes that much more important.

The subcommittee process should be formal, that is, it should not be ad hoc or taken lightly. Meetings should be held on a regular schedule, with a disciplined review of tasks required, to ensure that responsibility and accountability are established. Only through this approach can a conversion most effectively be completed within the time frames established, especially if it is a large system conversion.

DEVELOPMENT OF THE CONVERSION PLAN AND TARGET DATE

The conversion plan is similar to a project plan as a standard tool in project management. The purpose of a conversion plan is to document four key elements:

1. Task that must be accomplished.
2. Individual responsible for completing the task.
3. Target date for completion of the task.
4. Status of the task (open/completed, issues).

These elements are fundamental for any project or system conversion and can be quite lengthy. The conversion plan is the detailed blueprint of steps and tasks that must be accomplished to complete the conversion. As such there will be considerable detail. This is so because the document must incorporate every possible task required to be completed. An example of a typical conversion plan is illustrated in Figure 1.

Responsibility for Development and Maintenance

The overall system conversion coordinator is responsible for initially developing the conversion plan and for keeping it up-to-date. The initial development will be prepared in conjunction with other committee members to ensure that all necessary tasks are identified. Ongoing maintenance of the conversion plan involves physically changing the plan each time a committee meeting occurs and information is discussed regarding the items listed. Changes will typically consist of indications that a particular task is complete or recording issues under the "status" section of the plan indicating problems or other concerns that may be preventing satisfactory completion. Also, if the individual responsible is changed or target dates revised, these must be updated. It is through this type of updating that progress is made during the conversion. The conversion plan should be reviewed at each committee meeting for status updates.

Development of the Conversion Plan

The conversion plan itself, in addition to being formatted as in Figure 1, should be categorized. All tasks requiring completion should be arranged by the area of responsibility. In other words, tasks should be identified for the areas of: marketing, information systems, training, and each of the operational areas that are a part of the system conversion. The tasks should be recorded underneath each heading. In this way the committee member can easily focus on those tasks unique to the particular department. Furthermore this

Conversion Plan

Area:		Manager:				
Page: 1		Date Updated:				

ENVIRONS/ACTIVITIES	RESPONSIBLE	MEANS OF CHECK CUTOVER	TARGET START	TARGET END	ACTUAL END	STATUS

organization will facilitate matters when the subcommittee meets to discuss its own progress. An example of this type of structure is shown in Figure 2.

The conversion plan should be set up and maintained on a word processor for ease of update. It is important to be able to quickly and efficiently update the project plan for each meeting, regardless of frequency.

Once all tasks are identified, categorized, and recorded in the conversion plan format, the next step is to assign responsibility for each of the tasks. Responsibility for each task will usually be assigned to the subcommittee members for the corresponding broad category. This must be done in conjunction with each committee member and cannot be accomplished alone by the system conversion coordinator. The only portion of the conversion plan that is left uncompleted is the target date. This cannot be assigned until an overall conversion cutover date has been established.

Targeting the Conversion Date

The conversion date is the date on which cutover occurs from the old to the new system, from manual system to electronic system, or the addition or upgrade of a new software package is complete. Before the conversion plan can be completed, this date must be determined. The cutover date should allow ample time for the completion of all tasks. This can be determined from the service bureau (if outsourced) or the in-house data processing or information systems department. If this is an acquisition or merger, these departments will have a general sense of the time required to complete the tasks to effect the conversion. This will likely be expressed in weeks. If this is the case, the system conversion coordinator should count the number of weeks from the date the process is planned to begin and establish the cutover date. Cutover is the day that the bank will begin operating on the new system, combined system, or merged system. Usually this is the start of the week, a Monday. This allows the preceding

F I G U R E 2

Conversion Plan with Functional Categories

Area:		Manager:					
Page: 1		Date Updated:					
STEPS/ACTIVITIES		RESPONSIBLE	STATUS DISPLAY (AUTO/MAN)	TARGET START	TARGET END	ACTUAL END	STATUS
A. Voice Network							
1. Site visit/information gathering							
2. Plan telephone/PBX hardware needs							
3. Purchase telephone hardware/lines							
4. Installation of the PBX							
5. Telephone station reviews/programming							
6. Telephone handset placement							
7. Voice mail ID build/setup							
8. Activate phone/voice mail systems							
9. IVR programming							
10. Other voice network programming							
11. Activate IVR and other systems							

49

weekend (when the bank is closed) to be used for the final programming. This is not only highly desirable but vital to the process. Attempting to perform a system conversion cutover in mid-week would be detrimental to the process and would likely incur problems to which the bank could not easily respond.

When the conversion cutover date has been decided, it can be communicated to the system conversion committee members so that they can then establish target time frames for the completion of each of the tasks contained in the conversion plan. These dates, once established, should be communicated to the system conversion coordinator for inclusion in the overall conversion plan.

At this time the conversion plan can be completed. When the conversion plan is completed, the process can begin. An example of the completed conversion plan is shown in Figure 3. In some cases, the overall time required for the conversion may not be readily available from an information systems division or service bureau. If this is the case, it may be necessary for the system conversion coordinator to estimate the time required. This can be accomplished by using project management tools such as PERT (programmed evaluation and review technique) and/or CPM (critical path methodology). These are standard project management tools and are beyond the scope of this book. However, information on the use of these tools can be found in other project management publications or texts such as *Bank Systems Management* (K. Belasco) and *The Project Manager's Desk Reference* (James Lewis).

SUMMARY

In this chapter the primary focus has been to highlight the organization of the system conversion process. Care has been taken to outline how the system conversion process should begin from the identification of the scope through the targeting of the conversion date. Organizing the system conversion

FIGURE 3

Completed Conversion Plan

Area:	Information Systems		Manager: John Doe					
Page: 1			Date Updated: 11/28/95					

EVENT & ACTIVITIES	RESPONSIBLE	WEEKS BEFORE CUTOVER	TARGET START	TARGET END	ACTUAL END	STATUS
A. Voice Network						
1. Site visit/information gathering	Telecom. Manager	28	12/04/95	12/15/95		
2. Plan telephone/PBX hardware needs	Telecom. Manager	26	12/18/95	01/05/96		
3. Purchase telephone hardware/lines	Telecom. Manager	23	01/08/96	01/12/96		
4. Installation of the PBX	Vendor	13	03/18/96	03/22/96		
5. Telephone station reviews/programming	Telecom. Specialist	12	03/25/96	03/29/96		
6. Telephone handset placement	Vendor	12	03/25/96	03/29/96		
7. Voice mail ID build/setup	Telecom. Specialist	12	03/25/96	03/29/96		
8. Activate phone/voice mail systems	Vendor	10	04/08/96	04/08/96		
9. IVR programming	Telecom. Specialist	1	06/10/96	06/14/96		
10. Other voice network programming	Telecom. Specialist	1	06/10/96	06/14/96		
11. Activate IVR and other systems	Vendor	0	06/17/96	06/17/96		

51

process is, by far, the most important aspect of the conversion. For this reason detail has been provided to walk the reader through the various steps and tasks necessary to guarantee a successful conversion.

The chapter outlined the scope of the conversion, which defines the boundaries of what the conversion will and will not be. This is very important and will aid the conversion team in remaining focused on the primary mission, which is the system conversion. Of considerable importance is the establishment of the authority to proceed, including funding approval and identifying the appropriate resources needed to complete the system conversion. Top down commitment is vital because the process will involve existing personnel crossing numerous boundaries on a matrix management basis. A sponsor of the system conversion is an important part of the process, as the mentor or senior-level position will provide the authority to proceed as well as the communication point for issues and concerns.

The system conversion coordinator is the lead manager responsible for delivering the system conversion within the stated budget and at the date determined. The system conversion coordinator is the most important person involved in the process and, therefore, great care must be taken to select the right person to fill the position. Skills and characteristics were identified that are necessary for assisting the system conversion sponsor in identifying the right individual to fill the position of system conversion coordinator. During the selection process, two vital characteristics are of utmost importance—sense of urgency and an apolitical nature, with the ability to interact effectively with a wide range of people in various levels of the organization.

The conversion committee is the vehicle through which all tasks and functions will be completed during the process. The committee is made up of a core group of functional areas that would typically be involved in any type of conversion. In addition, operational managers or representatives will need to be a part of the committee to complete the tasks related to specific applications used by the bank. Subcommittees also are used to perform the tasks contained on the conversion plan. Subcommittees are chaired by the functional member who is a part of the overall conversion committee, to which periodic reports are presented by the subcommittee chair as to the progress made.

The final aspect of organization is the development of a detailed system conversion plan and cutover date. The conversion plan is broken down into functional area categories, with individual tasks contained under each. The conversion plan not only identifies the tasks needed to be completed but identifies the individual responsible for the completion of the task. The target time for the completion of the task cannot be established until a cutover date has been determined by the system conversion coordinator. Once this occurs, individual target dates can be assigned that will correspond to the timing in which the task must be completed in order to meet the cutover date.

Upon completion of the system conversion plan, the process is ready to begin. The organization and structure is now ready to commence the process and start working on each of the tasks contained in the conversion plan. At this point the personnel, time frames, and detailed blueprint have been completed, which allows the system conversion to commence in an orderly fashion.

CHAPTER 3

System Conversion Preparation

OVERVIEW

Preparation for the actual system conversion involves some thought and planning. The purpose of this phase is to develop the various mechanisms and processes to be used and carried out during the system conversion. The overall framework for the conversion is fashioned at this stage. Once the members of the conversion process are identified and the conversion plan completed, a number of tasks germane to managing and communicating the status of the system conversion can begin to be developed. This chapter will present in detail each of the preparatory functions necessary for ongoing coordination and management. The reader will become familiar with the following topics.

1. Preparation and development of the system conversion timeline and planning template.
2. Development of other project planning mechanisms.
3. Preparation and development of the agenda for conducting the kickoff meeting.

4. Development of meeting schedules, minutes and agenda format for future meetings, as well as how the meetings should be facilitated.

5. Executive summary reports, decisions, and communication mechanisms.

6. Work papers and documentation.

7. Assignment of responsibility to committee members and product leaders.

Each of the above is discussed in detail in the following pages.

PREPARATION OF THE CONVERSION TIMELINE AND PLANNING TEMPLATE

The system conversion timeline is a document used to display the overall time span required for the project displayed by key categories. The purpose of the document is to show where categories and tasks overlap, indicating the beginning and ending dates for the tasks that make up the broader category displayed. Timelines are generally completed in a standard document format know as a Gantt chart. The Gantt chart is a project management tool used by a number of different disciplines for planning and monitoring the timeliness of the project completion. In short the chart is used to monitor and evaluate progress in order to keep the project on a defined time frame and to ensure adherence to this schedule. Timelines are developed initially from information contained in the project plan identified in Chapter 2. The timeline itself, or Gantt chart, should not be as detailed as the project plan. Remember, the project plan contains the instructions, tasks, and detailed steps necessary for completion of the conversion, in all aspects. The timeline, on the other hand, captures key milestones or category headings and graphically displays the time span required or planned to complete all tasks that fall under the primary category. This timeline, when arrayed with others, illustrates where major categories of work overlap in addition to the time required. Figure 4 illustrates an example of a typical Gantt chart.

F I G U R E 4

Gantt Chart (timeline)

57

The timeline should be developed by the system conversion coordinator. When planning the systems conversion, it is often helpful to rough out a timeline by developing a template of the primary tasks required for completion. This template is developed without specific dates, but uses the number of weeks prior to the actual cutover date, or week zero, to indicate and plan the starting date of the system conversion process. Timeline templates are also very helpful in planning future bank acquisitions and the steps required for integrating them into the existing bank system.

The real benefit is the ability to overlay the template onto the current calendar to identify, relatively quickly, when the system conversion process must begin and end. This will also be helpful when planning the timing of future acquisitions, and as previously stated, is a definite goal when the bank is attempting to grow in the market through acquisition. In this case the competitive advantage is the ability to assimilate the new organization as rapidly as possible. Part of the assimilation process is the ability to quickly organize and convert the new acquisition to the bank's system.

Timeline templates should be organized around the major aspects involved in the overall system conversion. These include

1. Telephone systems.
2. Cabling.
3. Voice and data networks.
4. Microcomputers and local area networks.
5. Mainframe conversion.
6. Remote processing.
7. Training.
8. Communication.
9. Security.
10. Operations/procedure flow.
11. Disaster recovery.

Within each of the above categories, tasks are identified and plotted on the timeline, showing the time required from start to finish. The plotting of the timeline is based solely on the number of weeks to the system conversion cutover, not on actual dates. Dates are added to the timeline later after deciding when the process should begin and end. For example, if the bank must cable the branch of the acquiree for installation and activation of a local area network, enough time must be allowed to ensure proper installation and testing. Since cabling should be completed far enough in advance of system cutover to allow plenty of time for testing, installation and testing of microcomputers, and training of users, the time needed must be determined and plotted on the template. In our example this may be 10 weeks prior to cutover. An example of a timeline template is shown in Figure 5. In the example the reader will note that space is provided above the "weeks prior to cutover" section to fill in actual dates for planning purposes. The dates are usually the Monday of each week. This can be penciled in immediately above the "weeks prior to cutover" number and simply continued through the rest of the chart. In this way the system conversion coordinator can easily see when the process must begin and when it will end, taking into account the major tasks and the time required for them. If the bank's management is not certain when the acquisition will take place, the template can be used to create "what if" scenarios, to get an idea when the process must actually begin. This tool gives the bank the ability to predict accurately what to expect in virtually any conversion. This is especially helpful if the financial institution is planning ongoing acquisitions in the future.

The challenge, however, in accurately planning for system conversions is to develop an effective model or template. In many cases this cannot be accomplished unless the bank has considerable experience in such system conversions. However, the purpose of this book is to provide the reader with not only typical tasks in an overall system conversion but also the time (in weeks prior to cutover) required for an

F I G U R E 5

Timeline Template

60

effective system conversion. In other words the template is for planning the bank's next and/or future system conversions. The elements identified have been used in actual situations and are based on considerable actual experience by the writer. They are designed to assist the system conversion coordinator in planning the system conversion and knowing what tasks or elements must be considered.

The focus of the template assumes that the financial institution is acquiring an existing bank and must not only convert the major mainframe systems, but must also retrofit the physical branch or branches to the acquiring bank's technical standards. The elements presented must, in most cases, be considered in this scenario. However, it is possible that the acquiring bank does not have the systems that require this type of work. In this case the categories not needed can be omitted. Using the categories previously identified, the elements that must be considered within each are discussed in the next sections.

Telephone Systems

For new physical sites telephone systems must be considered to ensure that proper communication is compatible with the bank's communication methodology. The tasks and elements that must be considered along with time frames from cutover, are as follows:

	Task	Weeks Prior to Cutover
1.	Site visit and information gathering. What is the current telephone hardware, PBX, IVR, etc.	28
2.	Plan telephone and PBX hardware needs, as well as other business lines, modems, alarms, and IVR systems.	26
3.	Purchase/order telephone hardware, business lines needed, trunks, etc.	23

Task	Weeks Prior to Cutover
4. Installation of the PBX.	13
5. Telephone station reviews or handset programming and mapping of hunts, pickup groups, voice mail reverts, etc.	12
6. Telephone handset placement and connection/testing.	12
7. Voice mail ID build/setup.	12
8. Activate phone system, voice mail, and network functions (if available).	10
9. IVR (interactive voice response system) programming (if available) to the host for the new sites.	1
10. Other network/PBX programming as needed at the time of cutover.	1
11. Activate IVR and other systems.	0

Some of the above information may not apply to the bank at this time. However, the discipline may trigger other thoughts that are pertinent and merit consideration in the process. The purpose of the advance time in planning the telephone system conversion is that the newly acquired branches and staff will be unfamiliar with the acquiring bank's telephone systems. Because of this training will be required, not only on how to use the telephone hardware, but also the voice mail system and the established usage standards. Since this requires some time, it is highly desirable that users learn in advance of the mainframe system cutover so that the communication systems are in place when the cutover occurs. When a bank is acquired, the staff that survives will be required to learn many new systems, particularly the sales staff. The sales staff will not only need to learn a new telephone system, but also a different platform system that will likely require microcomputer skills and familiarity with new software. Understanding the new mainframe will also require training. Unfortunately, all of this training must occur prior to cutover. As a result, to the extent that training can be staggered, allowing time to assimilate the information is highly recommended. Later in this section a separate training chart is developed to consider all aspects of training.

Cabling

Cabling involves the wiring of the newly acquired facilities to permit access to both the new telephone system and microcomputers and local area networks. This, of course, depends on a number of assumptions. First the acquiring bank must have a local area network environment. Although this may be the case, fewer and fewer banks do not have microcomputers running in a local area network environment. Because telephone systems require some type of wiring, and since the norm is becoming fully networked environments, the assumption is that both voice and data cabling will be necessary for the new sites. Similar to the telephone system, the following tasks and time prior to cutover are displayed to provide readers with guidance for developing their own template.

	Task	Weeks Prior to Cutover
1.	Site visit and information gathering of location of staff for cabling purposes, and location of equipment closets or rooms.	28
2.	Obtain floor plans of every facility acquired. These should be basic drawings of the work floors indicating the location of staff, tellers, and other functions.	28
3.	Plan the installation of voice and data cable based on the telephone and microcomputer plans determined. This must include indications of where cable receptacles are to be placed and will require review by managers who know where staff will be located.	26

Task	Weeks Prior to Cutover
4. Order cabling from existing vendor, supplying floor plans and the total number of cable locations required.	23
5. Begin cabling sites and testing upon completion.	19

Cabling is critical to virtually all other technical installations, in that until cabling occurs telephone, voice network, local area network, and data network connectivity cannot occur. For this reason cabling must be planned well in advance and managed very closely to ensure precision in the commencement and on-time completion. Any delays in cabling, as will be illustrated more clearly in the next section of this chapter, will delay all other installations. This could cause the entire system conversion to become delayed or to get out of control. Because of this great care must be taken to make sure no deviations arise in this segment of the timeline once the schedule is established.

Another point of consideration is the testing and labeling of the cable locations. If the bank is familiar with and does quite a bit of cabling they may already be very familiar with this. However, words are never wasted when talking about a solid installation. This includes making sure that the cablers test the cable for connectivity as well as labeling all receptacles. Labeling is very important to ensure that it is known what device is connected to it for monitoring and troubleshooting.

Microcomputer/LAN Environment

Microcomputers and LANs are critical elements in the access of customer and mainframe data. Microcomputers provide the technical intelligence for utilization of a number of software tools in order to improve productivity and access to information. Today, most banks have considerable amounts of money invested in end-user computing systems. This has become more a way of life rather that leading edge technology. In order to plan and implement the local area network and microcomputers cabling must first be complete. Once this occurs the installation can occur. For the development of the timeline template there are a number of steps required for completion, these are outlined below:

	Task	Weeks Prior to Cutover
1.	Site visit and information gathering.	28
2.	Development of floor plans and locations of computers.	28
3.	Determine volume of hardware and software to be ordered.	23
4.	Place orders with vendors.	20
5.	Delivery and staging of computers and file servers/testing.	14
6.	File server configuration/installation.	12
7.	Microcomputer workstation/printer installation.	12
8.	Acceptance testing.	12
9.	LAN ID assignment and communication.	11
10.	End user training.	11

Microcomputers and LANs have become the new mainframes of today's information world. As a result the timing and installation of hardware and software is very important to the bank's ongoing success and future growth.

Voice and Data Network

Not all banks today have separate voice and data networks. Because of the number of bank conversions and combinations occurring, networking and network architectures have become strategic imperatives and are increasing in deployment. Voice and data networks are switching from analog to digital communications mainly 56 kbps and T-1 circuits. Since they are becoming more common and since most larger organizations use them, voice and data networks are discussed in this section.

Voice networks support interfacility dialing, the ability to centralize customer service or call centers, and other technical initiatives that may improve communication. This could include, for example, videoconferencing. The data network supports the mainframe communication (data) traffic that drives the bank's CRTs, teller machines, controllers, and microcomputers that are accessing host communications. In both cases they need to be planned in conjunction with the system conversion, particularly the data network, to ensure that mainframe communications to the new facilities are functioning at cutover. The tasks and time frames required for this category are outlined below.

	Task	Weeks Prior to Cutover
1.	Site visit and information gathering. This is necessary to determine what method the acquired facilities use for host or data and voice communications today.	28
2.	Plan both the voice and data network connectivity.	26
3.	Purchase voice circuits and hardware as well as data network hardware and circuits.	23
4.	Install data circuits and router and other hardware at all sites homed to the acquiring bank's host.	12
5.	Configure all data network routers to route data packets to the host as well as other sites if LAN-to-LAN traffic is to be used.	12
6.	Install voice network hardware and circuits.	12
7.	Program all PBXs to communicate with each site and test.	12

Task	Weeks Prior to Cutover
8. Activate network dialing for the voice network.	10
9. Test data network connectivity.	9
10. Activate data network connectivity.	0

As indicated, the voice network (if used) can be completed much sooner than cutover. There is no reason why the acquired bank staff cannot begin to used interfacility network dialing in advance. This not only will facilitate communication but will provide this level of communication at a time when attention can be devoted to it. The data network, on the other hand, cannot be handled in the same manner. The activation of LAN-to-LAN connectivity could occur sooner, but data communications to the host cannot occur until the banks are actually converted and cut over.

Mainframe

The mainframe system conversion is the most pervasive of the major categories of conversion that occur during this type of transition. The reason is that not only must it begin well in advance, but it will be completed after all other technical systems have been planned, installed, tested, and activated.

The mainframe system conversion involves the merging of information from the acquired financial institution to the acquiring institution's mainframe processor (whether in-house or outsourced). Of the identified technical conversion this requires considerably more tasks and activities over a period of time. In other words the time span from the onset to completion of these tasks is the longest. Mainframe conversion activities require a number of subtasks requiring completion during the process. The major tasks and weeks required prior to conversion are indicated below.

	Task	Weeks Prior to Cutover
1.	Conversion preplanning.	22
2.	Order duplicate account lists and review.	20
3.	Kickoff conversion meeting.	15
4.	Product mapping.	14
5.	System parameter change control.	14
6.	Application system programming.	11
7.	Receive/review test reports and make changes.	6
8.	Conversion weekend programming loading activation.	1
9.	System cutover.	0
10.	Application system balancing.	−1
11.	Month-end processing.	−4
12.	Conversion process termination.	−5

Remote Processing

Remote processing involves processing (bulk file and capture) of the bank's checks. This is an extremely important part of the operations and must be handled very sensitively. The first step is to determine whether the bank that has been acquired performs remote processing on the outside or in-house. If in-house, a decision must be made whether to continue this. If on the outside, a conversion will occur as will be the case if the decision is made to abandon the in-house processing. In either case care must be taken to ensure that the transition is smooth. The remote check processing function involves customer statement production as well as timely movement of checks to the bank's clearing agent. In one case the bank experiences a monetary impact, in the other, the bank's customers may be affected directly through delivery delays or inaccuracies. Furthermore, work must be transported to the remote site in some manner. This usually is done via courier once work has been proofed. This, as well as special handling situations, must be identified and coordinated and/or programmed into the new system to ensure uninterrupted processing. The basic steps involved in the process for consideration in the template are indicated below.

	Task	Weeks Prior to Cutover
1.	Site visit and information gathering.	14
2.	Information mapping and planning distribution of work, via courier, and special handling requirements.	12
3.	Remote site programming.	12
4.	Program installation and testing.	5
5.	Cutover and activation	0

Training

Training is pervasive during the entire conversion process. The reason for this is that training is required in a number of areas, which will be new to the employees being newly introduced to the systems. Unfortunately, with any system conversion, the conversion coordinator does not have unlimited time. Invariably, a cutover date based on the needs of the bank will be set. This is where the system conversion template is most helpful. Using the methodology previously discussed, training for the various areas is targeted, based on its proximity to the availability of the technology and to the conversion cutover. In other words, some training must be completed as close as possible to the cutover date simply because the change in the system will not and cannot occur until cutover. In this case, training should be conducted as close as possible to the cutover date to avoid erosion of information. In other cases conversion and training can occur well in advance of the cutover. An example of this is the conversion of the telephone system. If the newly acquired organization has an incompatible phone system, converting to the new telephone system can occur well in advance of the cutover. If this occurs as indicated training is accomplished at a time when it does not conflict with another form of training. It is always highly desirable to provide training on one set of technologies at a time, allowing time for practice and assimilation before introducing new information. It becomes somewhat of a juggling act to coordinate and schedule training for all areas so that time to adapt is built in. This kind of learning is best because it helps to imbed the information. This philosophy is employed in formal college programs and is the reason for lengthy semesters.

Training is required in each of the areas where new technology is added and/or changed. The sequence of this training is indicated below in the template information.

As indicated above, approximately four to five weeks is built into each new system to permit practice and deep learning. It is very important to focus on training needs as much as possible when developing the timeline template. Training is the one area that most often suffers in every transition. When projects are delayed or timelines are reduced, something must slip. Usually this is training. It is not omitted, but assimilation time may be greatly reduced.

	Task	Weeks Prior to Cutover
1.	Telephone/voice mail training.	10
2.	Microcomputer/LAN/and application software basic training.	8
3.	Mainframe application system training.	3
4.	Teller system training.	3
5.	Platform automation system training.	3
6.	Operational procedural flow training and handling.	1
7.	Refresher/follow-up training—all areas.	−5

Communication

Communication is hardly the last step in the process, and should not be thought so because it is discussed last. The fact is that communication is vital and must occur regularly and frequently throughout the process. Communication in a system conversion process has many different aspects. Customer communication comes to mind most frequently as a key element of communication. This includes notifications of service charge changes, hours of operation, services offered by the new entity, as well as what to expect during the transition process. Customer communications are absolutely vital during the conversion, simply because lack of communication or poor communication can cause customers to leave the bank or at least to consider it. Customers can be forgiving; however, when poor communication results from a system conversion, customers tend to become very concerned, seeing the conversion as the cause of current and future problems. This, in turn, can result in a lost customer. Communication, therefore, must be well planned and timed and occur throughout the conversion process. The items listed below identify the type of communication, in general, and when it should occur.

	Task	Weeks Prior to Cutover
1.	Duplicate account customer communications letter.	10
2.	Commercial/retail pricing disclosures and letters.	8
3.	ATM change communications (if applicable).	6
4.	Customer service and bank telephone number changes.	3
5.	General change communication letter, including potential outages, downtime.	2
6.	Change in daily cutoff time letter (if applicable).	2

As illustrated, time is required not only for the communication but also for mailing and handling responses to such communications.

Security

System security involves the planning and assignment of user identifications for access to mainframe application systems. Although in the past most system conversions involved only mainframe, given today's end-user systems and telephone communications, more than one type of security will be required. When building the timeline template advance time is required to plan and structure the type of security needed for the acquired organization. The security areas that must be considered in any full acquisition and conversion are outlined below.

	Task	Weeks Prior to Cutover
1.	Build voice mail IDs and communication.	12
2.	Local area network ID set up and communication.	9
3.	Build host (mainframe) user IDs and structure. Must determine level of access required.	11
4.	Communicate host user IDs.	2
5.	Test host user IDs.	1
6.	Activate host user IDs.	0

Operations/Procedure Flow

All system conversions, whether acquisition related or simply the conversion of microcomputer application software, require a change in procedures used by employees. Usually the reason the software was selected was to streamline or improve productivity. This cannot occur unless procedures change. In the case of a merger or new acquisition, procedures will certainly change for the acquired institution. The acquiror will, in most cases, rely on existing procedures to effect the acquisition with few changes to back office operations. However, in many merger environments, procedures and particularly work flows will likely be altered. This is extremely important and must be considered and planned so that once the conversion occurs the new procedures and work flows function as intended. Although this and the previous categories will be outlined in greater detail in a later chapter, the emphasis here is that planning must occur. For this reason operations/procedure flow must be included in the timeline template to ensure that time is taken to consider the issues involved. This is as important as system programming and the conversion itself, for if employees do not understand work flows and procedures, the conversion will be most difficult and fraught with error.

	Task	Weeks Prior to Cutover
1.	Develop outline of departments that are affected by the conversion.	25
2.	Develop flow charts of actual work flows anticipated for the current and postconversion environment.	23
3.	Highlight changes indicated in the flow charts and develop procedures and policy documentation for execution.	19
4.	Communicate changes to vendors and external parties to order new forms, equipment, and/or other services to be performed at conversion (place orders as need be).	10
5.	User critical review of procedures and cross-functional impact.	6
6.	Walkthrough of new procedures and work flows as well as vendor readiness check.	1
7.	Activation of new procedures and flows.	0

Greater detail is presented in later chapters to focus on specifics and how these work flows will be developed and in what areas. Again, the importance of planning for these tasks must not be deemphasized, as the success or failure of the conversion can rest on how smooth procedural transition occurs.

Disaster Recovery

Another area of consideration, often neglected, is backup systems and contingency planning. Major changes occurring from a merger or system conversion cannot happen without some effect on backup plans. When a new bank is acquired, how is it integrated into current disaster recovery plans, what allowances are made for network connectivity, what persons are involved in the backup planning, and how will this be co-ordinated? At the least, if the financial institution has a disaster recovery plan, it will or should go through major revision.

Unfortunately, this is not usually taken into consideration or well planned in the overall conversion process. To be certain this is addressed and to assure the organization that adequate backup exists once the conversion occurs, planning must be done. This planning must be a part of the overall process, and for this reason, is included in the timeline.

	Task	Weeks Prior to Cutover
1.	Gathering data on existing disaster recovery plans of the acquired organization.	28
2.	Integration of any existing plans to the acquiror bank plan.	25
3.	Review technical backup devices and plans for supporting the systems for the acquired entity, and establish adequate backup for: – Network. – Telephone. – LANs/servers. – Mainframe. – Remote processing. – Generators and UPS.	20
4.	Identify disaster team member changes as well as emergency call lists.	10
5.	Identify after-hours trouble reporting and action procedures.	9
6.	Update the disaster recovery manual, taking into account all changes.	8

Task	Weeks Prior to Cutover
7. Obtain management/board approval of revised plans.	4
8. Communication and distribution of revised plans and procedures for activation if needed.	2

That disaster plans are very important is highlighted most poignantly when the need to use them occurs. The bank owes it to the shareholders to ensure adequate disaster recovery and uninterrupted operations should such a disaster occur.

In general, the development of the timeline and timeline template for the system conversion is an immensely important aspect of the system conversion. This phase schedules and plans the duration of tasks, which, in turn, sets the boundaries for the temporary life of the system conversion. Using the detailed information presented previously, a completed timeline template can be developed. An example of this is contained in Figure 6. The last step is relatively easy. Using the completed timeline template, actual dates can now be recorded above the "weeks prior to cutover" to evaluate the overall system conversion in relation to calendar weeks. This can be accomplished by "what if" scenarios, that is, several scenarios or time spans can be developed and assessed for the optimum time compatible with the organization's objectives. When this is done, the document becomes the timeline used by the project committee for ongoing tracking and monitoring. An example of a completed Gantt chart is shown in Figure 7.

PREPARATION OF OTHER PROJECT PLANNING MECHANISMS

The object of this book is not to be a treatise on project management and tools but rather a focus on bank system conversions. Detailed explanations and discussions of other

FIGURE 6

Completed Timeline Template

WEEKS PRIOR TO CUTOVER

#	TASKS	RESPONSIBLE
A	**TELEPHONE SYSTEM**	
1.	Site visit and information gathering	
2.	Plan telephone/PBX hardware needs	
3.	Purchase/order telephone hardware	
4.	Installation of the PBX	
5.	Telephone station reviews	
6.	Telephone handset placement	
7.	Voice mail ID build/setup	
8.	Activate phone system	
9.	IVR programming	
10.	Other network programming	
11.	Activate IVR and other systems	
B	**CABLING**	
1.	Site visit and information gathering	
2.	Obtain floor plans of facility	
3.	Plan the install of voice/data cabling	
4.	Order cabling/approval	
5.	Cable installation	
C	**MICROCOMPUTER/LAN ENVIRONMENT**	
1.	Site visit and information gathering	
2.	Development of floor plans/PC locations	
3.	Determine order volume	
4.	Place orders	
5.	Delivery/staging of computers	
6.	File server configuration	
7.	Microcomputer/printer installation	
8.	Acceptance testing	
9.	LAN ID assignment/communication	
10.	End user training	

Week columns: 30 29 28 27 26 25 24 23 22 21 20 19 18 17 16 15 14 13 12 11 10 9 8 7 6 5 4 3 2 1 0 -1 -2 -3 -4 -5 -6 -7 -8

FIGURE 7

Completed Gantt Chart

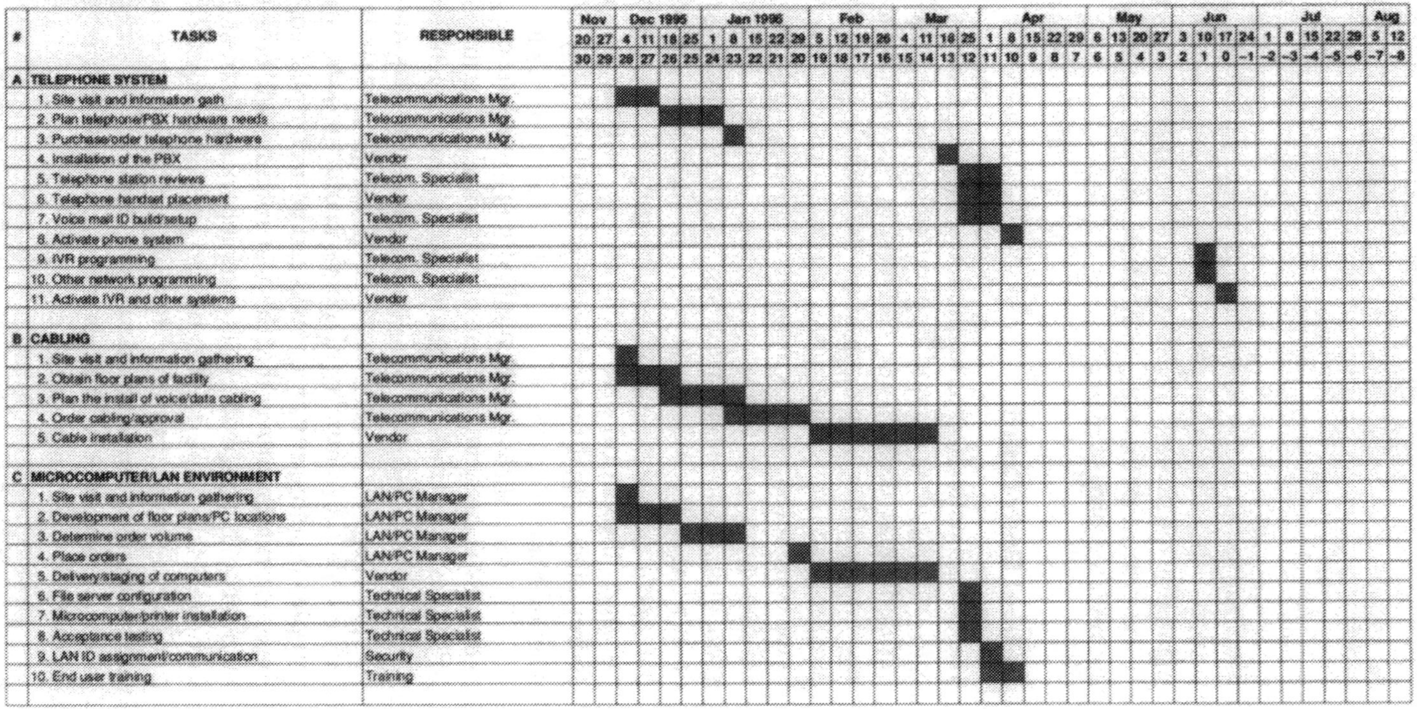

tools are beyond the scope of this book. However, a few project aids, when used properly, can be very beneficial to managing the process. The first, and most important, of these is the critical path chart. Others are project matrices and abbreviated project plans.

Critical Path Chart

The critical path chart or methodology (CPM) is a tool used to show relationships and dependencies. Its purpose is to highlight and clarify how conversion tasks relate to one another, whether they depend on the completion in a definite sequence or whether tasks can be done simultaneously. Once completed this document is very helpful to the conversion coordinator, the committee, and the conversion sponsor in mapping out what tasks must be completed first or in what order tasks must occur. In short, this is a project management planning tool. For the purposes of this book, however, the critical path methodology will be somewhat abbreviated so that the end result is simply developed and understood.

In reality, critical path methodology would occur prior to the development of the timeline. The reason for this is that CPM first identifies the relationships and dependencies, which helps to identify the time at which the task must be completed in relation to cutover. For example, if a particular task is critical to a number of others, in other words, must be completed before any other tasks can be accomplished, then the time prior to cutover that this task requires will be greater than those that depend on its completion. In contrast, tasks that are related but do not depend on one another can be completed simultaneously. The critical path exercise can be very helpful for understanding the entire process and gaining a deeper appreciation of the various pieces or tasks related to a given topic.

Development of the rudiments of a critical path analysis begins with the major categories involved in the system conversion. These are the 11 areas previously identified. For each category the tasks or subtasks associated with these are identified and arrayed. Using the information in the preceding section, as well as the weeks prior to cutover, a preliminary critical path chart can be developed. Remember, a critical path chart is a visual document. Its primary benefit rests with the ability to view relationships and understand dependencies. This will aid greatly in determining the relative importance of and proper emphasis on specific tasks to ensure their completion.

The information that goes into the development of the timeline template will suffice for the development of the critical path chart. When starting from scratch the number of weeks prior to cutover may not be readily known. In such cases the templates presented earlier can be used. However, to get to that stage one must first arrange tasks by category and determine how the tasks relate and what must occur before the next task can commence. For example, in order to plan the system and technical conversion when a new bank is acquired, one must perform a site visit. The site visit will identify what the acquired bank needs to become a part of the new organization. Since no tasks can even be started until an understanding of the environment occurs, all future work depends on the site visit assessment.

Few tasks, if any, can occur at the same time since it is not known at this stage what will be required. The only exception to this is the gathering of documents, forms, and such, as well as floor plans during the site visit. This task should occur simultaneously with the site visit to achieve the most efficient use of time.

A preliminary critical path chart can begin to take shape from the steps outlined above. This can be accomplished in a number of ways. The simplest is to develop an outline form, with tasks indented when they depend on the completion of a prior task. These later can be boxed for display in chart format. Classic critical path charts typically use circles or squares and tend to be very free-form in the array of the tasks, with connecting lines as the indicators of relationships and dependencies. This is, of course, acceptable but can make it difficult for individuals not familiar with classic critical path analysis. Figure 8 illustrates the preliminary development of this chart. Note that the boxed format helps to show relationships and dependencies in a relatively simple manner. The hierarchy form must remain true to the relationships of the tasks. In other words, as more tasks are added, they must be physically placed in relationship to what must occur before them. These, in turn, must remain consistent with prior tasks, and so forth. Ultimately, it is from this preliminary outline that time, in the form of weeks prior to cutover, will be assigned.

To summarize, one must review all major tasks relative to the conversion and simply begin to record them in this form, indenting as dependencies are noted. When the critical path chart is completed, the developer can begin to assign the time frames in terms of weeks prior to cutover. This must be consistent with where the task is arrayed in the overall outline. For ease of analysis and assignment, times can be recorded to the left of the document in a single column to correspond with the particular task. An example of a completed critical path chart, using the tasks already outlined in a typical conversion, is contained in Figure 9.

The critical path chart shown in Figure 9 can be used when planning the next acquisition/conversion, as the information contained is adapted from actual experience. Critical path analysis is a very important part of the system conversion in that it helps to clearly outline the impact of specific tasks. In the example (Figure 9) it is evident that cabling is a critical task because the installation of the telephone system, end-user system (LANs), and a wide-area data network cannot be accomplished if cabling has not occurred. Once cabling is completed, however, a number of tasks can be done simultaneously, tasks not on the critical path.

Critical path methodology can be very helpful in system conversions that are not as large or pervasive as the acquisi-

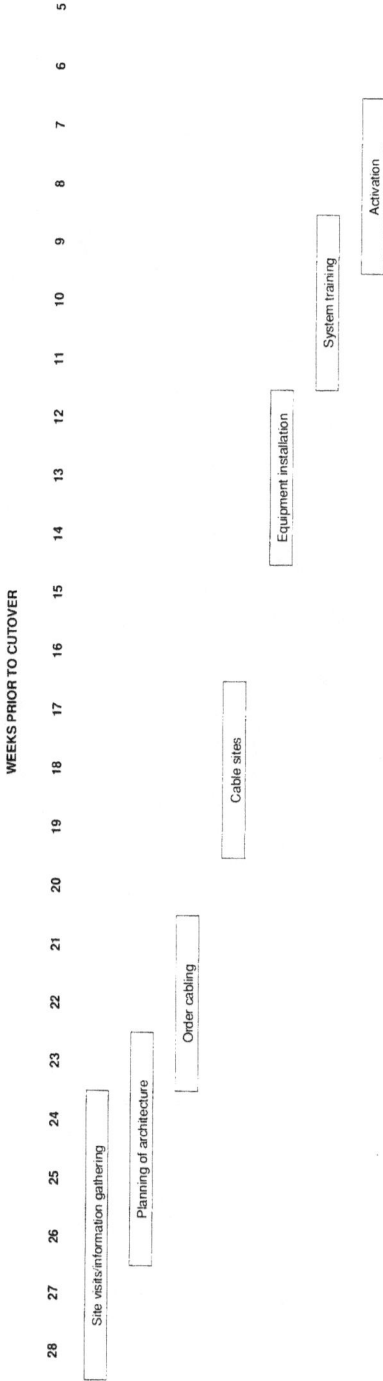

FIGURE 8

Preliminary Critical Path Document

WEEKS PRIOR TO CUTOVER

| 28 | 27 | 26 | 25 | 24 | 23 | 22 | 21 | 20 | 19 | 18 | 17 | 16 | 15 | 14 | 13 | 12 | 11 | 10 | 9 | 8 | 7 | 6 | 5 |

Site visits/information gathering

Planning of architecture

Order cabling

Cable sites

Equipment installation

System training

Activation

F I G U R E 9

Completed Critical Path Chart

WEEKS PRIOR TO CUTOVER

28 27 26 25 24 23 22 21 20 19 18 17 16 15 14 13 12 11 10 9 8 7 6 5 4 3 2 1 0 -1 -2 -3 -4 -5

- Site visits/information gathering
- Obtain floor plans
- Plan voice connectivity
- Plan data network connectivity
- Determine hardware software needs
- Plan phone-PBX hardware and needs
- Plan IVR disposition
- Plan ATM software changes
- Purchase voice circuits hardware
- Purchase PC hardware software
- Order cabling
- Order data network hardware
- Order telephone PBX hardware circuits
- Cable sites
- PBX Install
- Voice network install
- Phone station reviews
- Phone hardware install
- Build voice mail IDs
- Phone voice mail train
- Activate network dialing
- File server configuration install
- Microcomputer workstation prs. install
- System activation
- LAN ID set up
- Platform system installation
- PC LAN application software train
- Platform training
- Platform activation
- Teller training workstation installation
- Teller training
- Teller system installation
- Teller activation
- Install remote ATM circuits modems
- Router or parts ETIs configuration and install
- Testing
- Install ATM software test
- SNA Communication activation
- Cutover ATMs to network
- Conversion Programming
- Order duplicate account lists
- Kickoff meeting
- Product mapping
- System parameters
- Remote information gathering
- Remote programming
- Application programming
- Build host user IDs
- Test reports
- Communicate host user IDs
- Test host user IDs
- Conversion weekend
- Conversion programming
- System cutover
- Activate host user IDs
- Balancing
- Month end processing
- Conversion termination
- IVR upgrade programming
- Voice input PBX programming
- IVR Customer call activation

tion merger/conversion. When system upgrades, the installation of a new software package, or the development and programming of a new system are required, critical path methodology can be extremely beneficial in diagraming the process and understanding the critical nature of some tasks. This can help to organize the process so that timeline and other templates can be developed.

Other Tools

Other tools that can be employed during system conversions are graphic organizers such as matrices, which can highlight milestones or major tasks in an abbreviated manner. This type of documentation is beneficial when a large number of tasks and functions must be performed and the conversion coordinator seeks to break them down to more focused or manageable reports. This tool can be segmented by major category and used as a checklist for completion of key tasks. An example of this document is shown in Figure 10.

PREPARING FOR AND CONDUCTING THE KICKOFF MEETING

The kickoff meeting is the formal start of the system conversion process. It is formal in that all committee members are present, tasks are assigned and the process set in motion. Kickoff meetings are events, that is, they are themselves a milestone. Because of its importance, great care and attention must be taken in preparing for the kickoff meeting. Of most importance is establishing a sense of organization, control, and urgency. The tone set at this meeting will likely be carried throughout the entire process, and therefore it is vital that the meeting begin with the proper tone.

Preparation for the Meeting

Preparation for the kickoff meeting involves a number of vital steps. These are

F I G U R E 10

Task Matrix

TASKS	RESPONSIBLE	STATUS
MICROCOMPUTER/LAN PERIPHERALS		
1. Install software on network printers		COMPLETE
2. Order/obtain and install PCs		5/18/95
3. Order printers		5/18/95
4. Install printers		COMPLETE
5. Upgrade memory on file servers		6/5/95
6. Setup networked printers		6/12/95
7. Equipment delivery		6/12/95
8. File server setup and functionality		6/19/95
9. Identify additional equipment needs		6/19/95

1. *Develop a list of attendees.* Attendees needed for a kickoff meeting should be determined to ensure no critical members are absent. To omit key participants you run the risk of offending them as nonessential personnel. The attendee list should include the following individuals:
   - System conversion committee members (as previously defined in Chapter 2).
   - The CEO and/or conversion sponsor.
   - Other members of senior management.
   - Key third party vendors (if applicable).
2. *Determine the date, time, and place of the meeting.* The system conversion coordinator should set the date, time, and place of the kickoff meeting. It is necessary to check schedules of the participants to

ensure all will be able to attend. As ongoing meetings occur, the CEO, the conversion sponsor (if different), and senior management need not always attend. However, the kickoff meeting is not only the start of the process but a show of top down commitment and level of importance within the organization.

3. *Develop a meeting memo and agenda.* Once the meeting has been scheduled and all parties have been notified and attendance confirmed, an acknowledgment memo and agenda can be developed. The acknowledgment memo is a formal confirmation of the kickoff meeting time and place. This memo identifies what the meeting is, its purpose and logistics (date, day, time [start and end] and place). This formal reminder is vital to establish importance and ensure attendance. The acknowledgment memo is sent with an attached agenda for the meeting. The agenda is a key element in the overall process, particularly for the kickoff meeting. Elements that should be included in the kickoff meeting of the system conversion process are as follows:

   a. *Introductory remarks by the system conversion coordinator.* This is to re-establish the purpose of the meeting and to review the agenda. Any other housekeeping issues can be discussed during introductory comments.

   b. *Introductions.* The system conversion coordinator should introduce himself/herself and the key individuals present, such as the CEO and/or conversion sponsor as well as senior management. In addition the system conversion committee should introduce themselves with a brief comment on the role each will play in the conversion. Keep in mind that in the case of a new acquisition, key members of the acquired bank must participate in the conversion process and therefore will be present. In this situation introductions are extremely important because these individuals may not be known by members from the acquiring bank.

c. *CEO and/or conversion sponsor remarks.* The next portion of the meeting should permit the CEO and/or conversion sponsor (both if different) to comment on the system conversion effort about to begin. These remarks will anchor the process and establish the top down importance of the conversion, why it is being undertaken, and its importance to the livelihood of the bank. These remarks will charge the system conversion coordinator with the requisite level of accountability and responsibility for carrying out the process to the end.

d. *Review of timeline and targets.* After the opening remarks, the next point of communication should be a presentation of the timeline and target dates for the completion of the system conversion. The actual timeline should be distributed to the individuals present and should highlight key milestones—items critical to the process and the actual cutover date.

e. *Review of meeting schedule, format, and process.* The meeting schedule should be distributed, indicating a complete schedule through cutover. In addition the conversion coordinator should review the basic format of the meeting, flow, and documentation. This will include who will be attending the meetings on an ongoing basis as well as to how and when subcommittee meetings should be held.

     f. *Distribution of the project plan and discussion of the roles of committee members and subcommittees.* The detailed project plan, containing the actual tasks should be circulated to the attendees. An overview should be provided as to how tasks will be accomplished by whom and approximately when. This will include a discussion of the role of each committee member, the need to establish subcommittees and who will actually complete tasks, within what time frame.

    g. *Question and answer period.* This should be an open forum in which committee members can air concerns, issues, and items of clarification that will occur during the process. This is important to have while the CEO and other senior managers are present.

    h. *Begin the conversion meeting/assignment of tasks.* At this stage the CEO and senior managers may wish to leave. Now begins the formal conversion meeting with the committee members. It is not a full conversion meeting but rather a review of tasks required for completion, which are scheduled at this time. Identify tasks that have targets coming up soon and the start process. This portion of the meeting is not extensive and will normally be brief.

    i. *Adjournment/next meeting date.* The last part of the meeting is the formal adjournment and settling on a date for the next meeting.

Once the agenda has been completed, it can be attached to the cover memo acknowledging the meeting. This should be sent to all parties participating in the meeting. An example of the completed agenda will resemble the contents in Figure 11.

F I G U R E 11

Kickoff Meeting Agenda

Agenda	Individual
1. Introduction: – Meeting purpose – Review of agenda – Housekeeping issues	System conversion coordinator
2. Introductions: – System conversion coordinator – Conversion sponsor – CEO/President – Senior management – Conversion committee – Third party participants	System conversion coordinator
3. Opening remarks:	CEO/conversion sponsor
4. Review of timeline and target dates: – Cutover dates – Key milestones	System conversion coordinator
5. Review of meeting schedule, format, and process: – Time/date of meetings	System conversion coordinator
6. Project plan: – Review of plan – Review of committee roles	System conversion coordinator
7. Questions/answers: – Open discussion	All
8. Conversion meeting beginning: – Assignment of tasks – Status discussion	System conversion coordinator
9. Adjournment/next meeting: – Scheduling next meeting – Other issues – Closing remarks	System conversion coordinator

Conducting the Kickoff Meeting

In the section on identifying the agenda, a fairly detailed account of what occurs at the kickoff meeting was provided. Kickoff meetings should be succinct, and not a marathon. As stated previously, the kickoff meeting should be viewed as an event and conducted accordingly. The system conversion coordinator should keep the meeting moving and maintain an upbeat, enthusiastic atmosphere. A primary purpose is to energize the personnel present and motivate them to go forth and complete the system conversion. It is important that the meeting be conducted using these tips. Most system conversions for newly acquired banks are relatively lengthy processes, with much work to be conducted. It should also be recognized that the members still have a day-to-day job to perform for the bank. Conversion duties are add-ons to this workload. Because of this, the system conversion must be communicated in a fashion that charges people, not burdens them with additional work.

Preparation for this and other conversion meetings is an important aspect of the overall process. Time must be made available by the system conversion coordinator to adequately prepare for the kickoff meeting. Ill-prepared or poorly-conducted kickoff meetings send a message that the process will likely not be smooth, will be disorganized, and could, in fact, create more problems and work. The success of the conversion depends greatly on how well the system coordinator can demonstrate organization, flow, and urgency. If he or she is successful in this, the system conversion will likely be very successful.

DEVELOPMENT OF MEETING SCHEDULE, MINUTES, AGENDA FORMAT, AND MEETING FLOW

Ordinary committee meetings, like the kickoff meeting, must follow an orderly routine to be efficient. They should follow a relatively standard agenda from which reports are made and progress is reviewed. Standardization of the agenda establishes a structure that ensures that all aspects of the conversion are discussed and reviewed on a timely basis.

As is often the case with system conversions involving mergers or acquisitions, the volume of work is substantial. No one person can do it alone. Furthermore, because of the detail involved and the ramifications of the decisions made, it is critical that continual review occur. For example, if an extremely critical task must be accomplished which, if not completed, could jeopardize the entire system conversion, review of this task for status updates and concerns should occur at each meeting. This applies to any objective that cannot be accomplished overnight. When an individual decides to lose weight and embarks upon a diet regime, the goal cannot be accomplished in one day. It will take weeks. However, the objective will not be met if there are no periodic reviews of progress via the scale. One cannot hope to lose many pounds over a period of time without monitoring progress regularly along the way. In the same way the volume of tasks cannot be completed, within the time frame desired, without status updates at frequent intervals to ensure that nothing is prohibiting the attainment of the objective.

Schedule

According to the above logic, system conversion committee meetings must be scheduled, in advance, on a consistent, frequent basis. The interval between committee meetings should be in the range of two weeks or less, depending on how much time is involved in the entire system conversion process. A system conversion that requires more than one year may have monthly meetings. Conversions needing less than one year but more than six months should have committee meetings every other week. Conversions lasting less than six months should probably have a meeting every week. Frequency should be related to the consequences of not completing a given task. If the system conversion is of short duration, the consequences of an uncompleted task could be severe if not known for a month or so. Lack of timely follow-up could delay the conversion—not a desirable outcome.

Most system conversions fall within the six-month or longer time frame. As a result the meeting interval should be approximately every two weeks. Once this is determined, a meeting schedule should be developed for the duration of the system conversion and distributed at the kickoff meeting. This not only establishes the order required, but also provides an advance schedule from which participants can allocate time. The short interval ensures that if a key task is not completed on time, no more than two weeks would pass before action is taken. There is usually enough time to get the task on track before any permanent schedule damage is done.

Minutes

Minutes are very important in the system conversion process. Minutes are the documented actions and discussions that occur during system conversion meetings. It is desirable that an independent party, not the system conversion coordinator or committee participants, take the minutes. This could be a secretary or administrative assistant who has done this before. Minutes need not be verbatim; therefore, tape recordings are unnecessary. Part of the reason for this is that minutes should be taken at every committee meeting. If committee meetings are held every two weeks, very detailed minutes would likely not be completed far enough in advance of the next meeting to be read. Hence, they would lose their value. Because of this it is strongly recommended that minutes be taken in the form of bulleted statements capturing key pieces of information or areas of concern. When a task is reported as completed, it is not vital that this appear in the written minutes, because task completion will be indicated on the project plan.

Minutes should be clear, concise, and in the form of line items (sentences not paragraphs). Minutes from board meetings and other more formal gatherings tend to be narrative and in the form of paragraphs. This is acceptable for meetings that occur every three months or so, but not for system conversion meetings that occur every other week. Properly kept minutes can be very helpful in developing the agenda and conducting the flow of the meeting. In this regard, system conversion committee meeting minutes should follow these guidelines:

1. Record promises of action with dates.
2. Record problems requiring completion with dates and individuals responsible.
3. Record items requiring decisions from a higher authority, regarding policy or other customer impact.
4. Record open issues where no resolution is immediately available and that require further discussion and research.

Agenda

The agenda for the regular conversion committee meetings should be unvarying from meeting to meeting. The agenda should set forth the order in which discussions, reviews, and actions will proceed during the meeting. Since meetings occur within short intervals of time, it is not productive to devote hours of time to the development of detailed agendas, as may have been spent for the kickoff meeting agenda. Since the agenda is standard for each meeting, it can be recopied and distributed at every meeting, with attached materials. For most system conversion meetings, the standing agenda should contain the information outlined below.

1. Review of timeline and time remaining to key milestone dates or cutover.
2. Review the outstanding issues list and discussion.
3. Review of the project plan and upcoming tasks for completion and discussion.

4. Other issues/questions.

5. Adjournment/next meeting reminder.

The agenda is succinct. It is not necessary that it be changed for each meeting. The next section outlines what supporting information is reviewed at the meeting and how the meeting is conducted.

Conversion Committee Meeting Format and Flow

Preparation for each upcoming system conversion committee meeting should begin soon after the last meeting. The primary role of the system conversion coordinator is to manage the process, follow up and remove barriers, not to perform the tasks. This is important because if the system conversion coordinator becomes bogged down with tasks to perform, he or she will not devote the time needed to evaluate the status of key tasks and make sure that true management occurs. Throughout any system conversion process will be a need to escalate issues, remove barriers, run interference, or simply to emphasize urgency. All of which requires time and attention to be successful. In this regard the system conversion coordinator must prepare for each meeting by performing the following tasks:

- Review/transcribe minutes into outstanding issues list.
- Update project plans.
- Update timelines.

Review/transcribe minutes into outstanding issues list. Previously it was mentioned that minutes should be short and succinct, limited to key pieces of information. Whoever has responsibility for taking down the information delivers these, once completed, to the system conversion coordinator. The system conversion coordinator reviews each and develops a list of outstanding issues for discussion at the next meeting. The purpose of this is to reduce the minutes further, to actionable items. In this way if minutes are distributed immediately prior to the next meeting, there is no urgency to read them in detail because the key aspects will be reflected in the outstanding issues.

The minutes, themselves, are still included in the information distributed to all committee members. However, they are more archival than integrated into the meeting process. This is beneficial because the detailed minutes will be referenced from time to time to clarify points or to understand what had transpired at a previous time. As previously stated, the review of these outstanding items is an element in the standing agenda.

Update project plans. The project plan was developed early in the system conversion process. The project plan is the reservoir of all tasks, targets, individuals responsible, and status of each item. If properly managed this becomes a permanent record of the system conversion similar to a blueprint. Whenever a system conversion committee meeting is conducted, the agenda calls for a review of the project plan. The project plan is reviewed in conjunction with the tasks due, as of the meeting, as well as a review of any tasks that remain outstanding and have been delayed. As each committee member addresses the status of each item, the system conversion coordinator should record the changes directly on the latest update of the project plan. After the meeting the project plan can be formally updated using whatever software package is preferred to produce updates. Project plan updates should be made at the end of every meeting with new/updated project plans distributed at the next committee meeting. By maintaining this level of discipline, every committee member will be completely up to date on all pertinent tasks and issues. Failure to maintain project plans in an up-to-date status can cause confusion and can even cause people to duplicate work that may already be completed. For these reasons project plan updating is a vital ingredient in the overall success of the management of the system conversion process.

Update timelines. In addition to the project plans, the timeline (Gantt chart) should be updated on a regular basis. Having the timeline preformatted using either a project management software package or other software will help to speed the update process and ensure the latest information. As discussed earlier, timelines need not be as detailed as the project plan. The purpose of the timeline is to show the time required for a particular category of activities and how it relates to other key categories of activities.

Since the timeline is an element in the agenda, it is important to be as up to date as possible. At the completion of each meeting, and before the next committee meeting, the system conversion coordinator should review the updated project plan and assess whether the category of activities reflected in the timeline has been completed or not. In this regard the system conversion coordinator will update the timeline when it is appropriate to do so. Updates to timelines can be reflected, graphically, in many ways. Using a spreadsheet software package lends itself to shading the time bars. Other more professional project management software uses other symbols to display progress or lack thereof. In all cases three basic concepts must be shown, activities scheduled, activities completed, and activities that have slipped. Activities scheduled simply are the initial bar lines that illustrate the span of time allotted or scheduled for the activities. This was shown in Figure 7. Activities completed are displayed by either darkening the line or using other symbols to clearly differentiate them from others. Completed activities should be prominently marked not only to differentiate it from others but to visually show progress at a glance. Psychologically, the updating of completed activities is an accomplishment, and displaying it for all to see can bolster motivation by showing that progress is being made. Last, activities slipped are reflected in some manner that shows that the timeline has been extended for some reason. This is done so that at any point in time it is apparent which activities have been delayed. Part of the reason for illustrating this is to draw attention and a sense of urgency to these activities so that energies are focused on their timely completion. The chart itself indicates the meaning of symbols or shading by way of a legend at the bottom of the page. In this way even the casual reader can see, at a glance, what the status of the system conversion is. An example of a timeline that reflects these elements is shown in Figure 12.

Conducting the Periodic Committee Meeting

The conversion committee meeting held every other week should be an efficiently conducted and facilitated meeting simply because everyone has much to do. In this regard the standing agenda, previously outlined, dictates the order in which the meeting will flow. Within each of the agenda items are a few additional concepts that require mention: (1) *The review of the timeline,* usually first, provides the committee with a sense of time and emphasizes the temporary nature of the system conversion. The timeline is a reference point to indicate to the committee members how close they are to the cutover and to trigger further efforts or energy necessary to meet the time frames. Reviewing this at every meeting provides a base from which all discussion should emanate. (2) *The review of the outstanding items list* provides a tracking of what was promised, what issues require discussion and resolution, and what items are problems. The committee member responsible for the item should address progress. This can be accomplished by a report from that individual or, if appropriate, a subcommittee member may wish to attend the committee meeting to provide more detail or clarification of the issue. Although subcommittee members for key areas normally would not attend the standing conversion committee meeting (this could make the meeting unwieldy) they nevertheless can be invited to attend when their expertise is required or can further clarify the issue. Outstanding issues, by definition, may be issues more troublesome than routine ones. Because of this there

Completed Gantt Chart

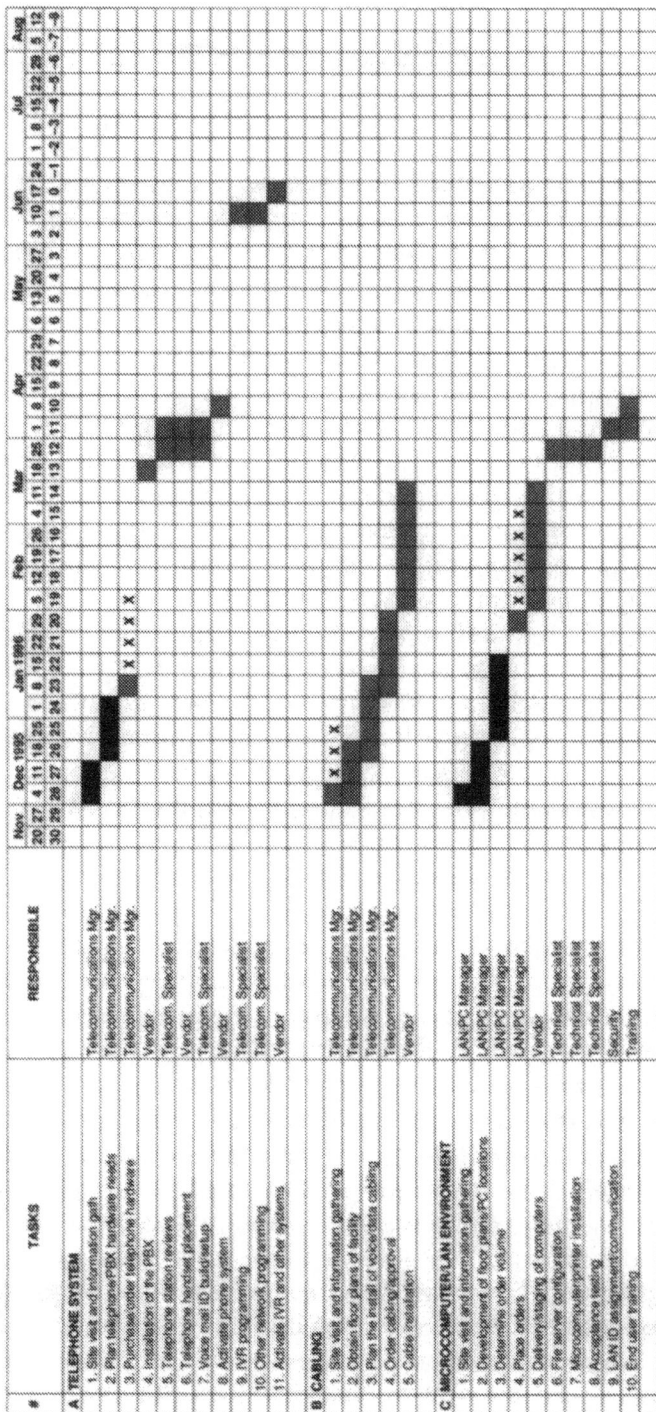

#	TASKS	RESPONSIBLE
A	**TELEPHONE SYSTEM**	
1.	Site visit and information gath	Telecommunications Mgr.
2.	Plan telephone/PBX hardware needs	Telecommunications Mgr.
3.	Purchase/order telephone hardware	Telecommunications Mgr.
4.	Installation of the PBX	Vendor
5.	Telephone station reviews	Telecom. Specialist
6.	Telephone handset placement	Vendor
7.	Voice mail ID build setup	Telecom. Specialist
8.	Activate phone system	Vendor
9.	IVR programming	Telecom. Specialist
10.	Other network programming	Telecom. Specialist
11.	Activate IVR and other systems	Vendor
B	**CABLING**	
1.	Site visit and information gathering	Telecommunications Mgr.
2.	Obtain floor plans of facility	Telecommunications Mgr.
3.	Plan the install of voice/data cabling	Telecommunications Mgr.
4.	Order cabling/approval	Telecommunications Mgr.
5.	Cable installation	Vendor
C	**MICROCOMPUTER/LAN ENVIRONMENT**	
1.	Site visit and information gathering	LAN/PC Manager
2.	Development of floor plans PC locations	LAN/PC Manager
3.	Determine order volume	LAN/PC Manager
4.	Place orders	LAN/PC Manager
5.	Delivery/staging of computers	Vendor
6.	File server configuration	Technical Specialist
7.	Microcomputer/printer installation	Technical Specialist
8.	Acceptance testing	Technical Specialist
9.	LAN ID assignment/communication	Security
10.	End user training	Training

Timeline columns: Nov (20/27, 30/29), Dec 1995 (4/27, 11/28, 18/25, 25/24), Jan 1996 (1/23, 8/22, 15/21, 22/20, 29/19), Feb (5/18, 12/17, 19/16, 26/15), Mar (4/14, 11/13, 18/12, 25/11), Apr (1/10, 8/9, 15/8, 22/7, 29/6), May (6/5, 13/4, 20/3, 27/2), Jun (3/1, 10/0, 17/-1, 24/-2), Jul (1/-3, 8/-4, 15/-5, 22/-6, 29/-7), Aug (5/-8, 12/-9)

Task scheduled
Task completed
X X X X X X X X Tasks slipped

is likely to be considerable discussion of these items. At this point the skill of the system conversion coordinator as a facilitator will be challenged. He or she must be able to move the conversion along, while permitting discussion, so that a course of action is ultimately taken. It is very easy to spend a considerable part of the meeting time in discussion with no direction determined unless guidance is provided. Review of outstanding issues will likely require more time than any other on the agenda. (3) *The project plan review,* which is next on the agenda, is more regimented and organized. This is a walkthrough of the project plan soliciting feedback from committee members on the tasks and activities scheduled for completion before the next scheduled meeting. In addition information is supplied about the activities that were to have been completed over the preceding two weeks. Again, it is important to be efficient to move the meeting along but also to uncover important issues that may become barriers to the successful completion of the activity. This may require some probing on the part of the system conversion coordinator as well as a keen sense when to interject himself or herself into the workings of the subcommittee to assist in completion of the task. (4) *The last part of the meeting is open-ended* in that other issues or questions can be raised that may not be appropriate at other times. These can be issues related to the process, the constitution of members of the committee, or any other ancillary issues. In all cases the meeting should not drag on from this point but should continue to remain crisp and succinct.

Coordination of the every-other-week committee meetings, as one might guess, is an important event in the life of the system conversion process. Meetings are the points at which the system conversion is truly managed. The purpose for coming together frequently is to obtain a status, address issues, get items back on track, remove barriers, and go on about the business of completing activities. In this regard the system conversion coordinator must be forever cognizant of time and demands placed upon the committee members. Well run, efficient meetings greatly add to the organization of the system conversion and help to ensure a quality outcome.

EXECUTIVE SUMMARIES, COMMUNICATION, AND DECISIONS

System conversions do not operate independently but rather are accountable to some governing body. This usually is the executive committee of the bank, in particular, the CEO and/or system conversion sponsor. The involvement of this group actually begins with the conversion sponsor but is formally initiated with the kickoff meeting. Throughout the process, however, the executive team must be involved at least to understand key issues and know the general direction and progress of the system conversion. This is accomplished in a number of ways and focuses on three primary areas: (1) summary level reporting, (2) general communications, and (3) policy decision making.

Summary Level Reporting

Summary level reporting refers to abbreviated information pertinent to a senior management group. During the course of the system conversion, much information and documentation are developed and circulated. In the preceding section, minutes, project plans, and timelines were discussed, with updates being produced every two weeks. Generally, to keep senior management informed of the progress of the system conversion process, it is always good policy for the system conversion coordinator to discuss what information the senior management group would like to see, when and how often, with the CEO and/or system conversion sponsor. However, in the absence of such discussion, most senior executives will likely desire to see less than more. Since a considerable volume of information will be produced during the course of the system conversion, it is most beneficial to target intervals at which reports will be delivered to this group. This may not be as frequent as every other week. Monthly reporting may suffice for keeping the senior management group informed of the conversion process. In addition to this level of frequency, the format of the reporting will likely be different. In almost all cases, the two documents most beneficial to the senior management group will be the updated timeline and synopsis of issues or minutes. The project plan is much too detailed for this group to be concerned with. In this regard the timeline can be reproduced from the standard package of materials and a synopsis of outstanding issues developed. The outstanding issues would not necessarily be the same list included in the agenda. It would be a separate report that summarizes some of these issues and translates them into a few "bullets". The purpose of this type of communication is to provide adequate overview information in as few words as possible. To accomplish this, the system conversion coordinator could organize the report to reflect a few key categories:

- Issues requiring decisions.
- Critical issues that remain open.
- Assessment of progress to date.

Issues requiring decisions. During the course of the system conversion, a number of circumstances will occur that require a decision from a governing body. In other words, these issues are beyond the scope of the system conversion committee. These issues involve pricing decisions, product offerings, advertising and external communication, and other cost-related issues. When these surface at the system conversion committee meeting they must be answered. The resolution of these issues involves documenting the items and transferring them to another level for timely resolution. Although the mechanics of this will be discussed later in this section, summary reporting is an appropriate place to communicate such information.

Critical issues that remain open. From the outstanding issues list, a number of questions may surface for which there is no answer. The purpose of the committee is to assign responsibility and obtain timely answers. However, this may not occur immediately. To ensure that they are not over-looked and forgotten, such issues must remain as outstanding items not only in the agenda of the committee but also in the summary report to the executive committee. Senior managers should always be made aware of the troublesome issues deemed critical to the process. Communicating these issues in the summary report can elicit assistance and support for their resolution. At the least, an awareness is created of the sensitive nature of the items. In this way there are no surprises to get in the way of the progress of the committee. Reflecting such items in the report to the senior managers is not merely recopying the outstanding items from the committee agenda. Rather, an assessment is made as to which items are critical to the process and must be communicated. To define the nature of criticality, the system conversion coordinator should report any outstanding item that could jeopardize the conversion or a key aspect of the conversion if it is not resolved on a timely basis.

Assessment of progress to date. This section of the summary report is the system conversion coordinator's own comments about what he or she believes is the progress of the system conversion. This section should be brief but provide accuracy and clarity in its reporting. If the timeline reflects much slippage, the system conversion coordinator should communicate the general cause of such slippage and what is being done to get things back on track. Furthermore, if slippage is an issue, the system conversion coordinator should communicate whether the conversion is in jeopardy and can be corrected.

In general, the system conversion coordinator should strive to be as succinct as possible, providing information that gives a fair assessment of the progress without inundating the senior managers with mounds of data.

General Communications

General communications, beyond the summary level reporting, will not likely be extensive with the senior management group. For the most part communications will be between the conversion sponsor and the system conversion coordinator. However, as the system conversion process progresses, situations will arise at committee meetings that will require some form of escalation to other senior level executives. Many times during the conversion process an issue will cross a number of boundaries or will be impeded by another area of the bank. In these circumstances the only method of completing the task may involve escalation and/or negotiation with senior managers responsible for the area. Part of the job of the system conversion coordinator is to function as a liaison and mediator, if necessary, to move the process along. This is not a negative occurrence and one that indicates the process is off track, but merely a fact of life. Invariably, system conversions will delve into all areas of the bank at some time or another. When this occurs friction can and will occur when the objectives of the conversion clash with the objectives of running a bank. In these circumstances it is the role of the system conversion coordinator to develop an understanding of the issues and seek out the senior manager ultimately responsible for the department to ask her or his assistance in resolving the issue. Remember the purpose for inviting the senior executives to the kickoff meeting was to establish commitment to the system conversion, for them to see firsthand the objective of the system conversion and to buy into it. Since the preliminary work was done by the system conversion coordinator it should be relatively easy for him or her to approach the senior executive and solicit help. In other words, the door has already been opened, which should permit prompt resolution of the issue.

One might be concerned with escalation of issues to senior level executives, due to possible negative repercussions. However, system conversions, especially large, pervasive conversions as in a bank merger or acquisition, are temporary and governed by time. Because of this little time is available to have issues become mired in politics or turf issues. The goal is prompt and efficient resolution so that the committee can continue unimpeded. Again, this is a very important role of the system conversion coordinator and one that should not involve hesitation when confronted with a blockage.

Policy Decision Making

The last area of executive communications is more formal. Throughout the system conversion process decisions will need to be made that are beyond the scope of the system conversion committee. Typically these occur during acquisitions and mergers. As the process continues, issues such as pricing and product-related and customer communications will arise that will necessitate executive involvement. Issues that arise will do so during the system conversion committee meeting. When this occurs there must be some method of surfacing and transferring issues to the executive committee or decision-making body for a prompt decision. When the system conversion committee is initially established, the system conversion coordinator should work closely with the system conversion sponsor to establish the flow of issues to him or her for presentation to the executive committee. In other words, the conversion sponsor is generally the entree into the executive committee. Unfortunately, executive committees seldom meet frequently enough to serve the purposes of the system conversion committee and process. As a result a process must be established that can activate an ad hoc executive committee meeting to make decisions on a timely basis. To establish this, the conversion sponsor can and should be instrumental. It will involve communications with the CEO and other senior executives to develop a process by which the issue can be promptly sent to the group and for which a decision can be expected within a relatively short time. It is very important to the process that this establishment not be taken lightly. The process by which issues are delivered and acted upon must be formally established with some guidelines for quorums in the event all members are not available. If this is too informal, difficulty will occur in getting decisions made, which will delay the conversion. This can put the control of the conversion timeline outside of the system conversion coordinator. In some conversions a special executive committee meeting is established for the purpose of reviewing conversion progress and to make timely decisions. It can be a regularly scheduled monthly meeting, anticipating the presentation of issues that require discussion and direction. This, by far is the most effective methodology and the one recommended. If this cannot be established, then it is very important for the system conversion coordinator to ensure that continual communications occur with the conversion sponsor to alert him or her of issues that may be surfacing and to request that the executive committee be alerted. The summary level reporting, previously discussed, identified a section of this report listing issues which require decisions. This is very effective when a standing monthly meeting, or at least, a frequently scheduled executive committee meeting has been established. In this regard the summary level reporting not only will apprise the group of the system conversion process but serves as a vehicle for documenting decision points. This then makes the process more organized and efficient and will likely guarantee that decisions will be made rapidly.

WORK PAPERS AND DOCUMENTATION

The system conversion coordinator plays another role in the conversion process. This role is record keeper and documentation storage. For every system conversion a conversion file must first be developed by the coordinator. The purpose of the file is to document and record all pertinent information related to the system conversion for referral and historical documentation. In many ways this process mirrors that of an internal or external auditor. Auditors are notorious for building and maintaining detailed files during a particular audit. These not only are well organized but generally are chronologically arranged. The system conversion is no different. Work papers are vital to the process and are used for building a record of what transpired, to develop a model of information for future system conversions, and to develop a point of reference for issues requiring research that occur during the process.

Work papers and documentation are most effective when well organized and easy to use. The work papers or conversion file should be maintained by the system conversion coordinator and should include the following sections and information:

- Timelines and critical path charts.
- Project plans (updated).
- Meeting minutes.
- Agendas and outstanding issues.
- Executive decisions, reports, and communications.
- Memos, notes, and other documents.

The system conversion coordinator should set up a binder or file folder with sections (leafs). The file folder approach, similar to a credit file for commercial bank lenders, is more versatile and highly recommended. Six sections should be labeled with the categories listed above.

Timelines and critical path charts. The initial timeline, timeline template, and critical path chart (if used) should be placed in this section. As the timeline is changed, the most up-to-date timeline (Gantt chart) should be at the top for ready access at each system conversion committee meeting. It is important that no other documents be placed in this section of the conversion folder, so that the most current chart is readily accessible. Furthermore, when researching information at later dates, the time frame should be easily accessible.

Project plans. The project plan, as previously identified, is the detailed blueprint of the system conversion process containing all tasks and activities required to be completed. This section of the folder should contain the most recent project plan for access and review during the conversion meeting. Previous project plans are not necessary to maintain at each update. Only the most current project plan should be in this section.

Meeting minutes. Each committee meeting will have minutes from the most recent session. Each time these are produced and delivered, they should be kept in this section of the file folder. In this case, however, it is important to keep all previous minutes in the same section. The most recent meeting minutes should be placed at the top of this section of the folder with all previous minutes underneath. Past minutes are important documents not only during the conversion process but afterward as well. Often, it is necessary to refer to what was said or agreed upon at a given meeting. The meeting minutes are a permanent record of issues discussed, decisions made, and other elements outlined. These documents will be most instrumental in gaining a complete understanding of the entire system conversion process at any point in time.

Agendas and outstanding issues. As discussed previously, standing agendas are recommended for all system conversion meetings. The agenda includes the outstanding issues list developed from the meeting minutes and to be discussed at the conversion committee. Similar to the meeting minutes, all past agendas and outstanding issue lists should be kept in the folder for future reference. The most recent agenda and outstanding issues list should be first in the folder section.

Executive decisions, reports, and communications. In this folder section all summary reports to the executive committee, or governing body, should be retained. These include any responses from the executive committee to outstanding issues requiring decisions. This is a permanent file and should include all past summary reports as well as any decision-related responses from the executive group. Particularly in this section, frequent referral may be made to past decisions or reports to ensure that the decision was correctly applied to the process. By maintaining these records in a separate section, ready access is permitted, which will facilitate organization and control.

Memos, notes, and other documents. The last section of the conversion file should contain any memos pertinent to the system conversion. This section is a receptacle for all information deemed beneficial or important to the process. Additionally, this could include schedules, test report results, system documentation, or notes from system conversion committee meetings. Since the file can become relatively large if the conversion is pervasive, care must be taken to ensure that unnecessary documents be kept out of the file folder.

Although the system conversion coordinator should maintain a file folder in this order for ongoing and future reference, each member of the system conversion committee should also develop and maintain a similar file. To the extent that the conversion file of the committee member and system conversion coordinator mirror one another, effective communication and organization will occur. Each committee member should also have a second file folder, for all subcommittee meetings. The system conversion committee member functions as the coordinator of the subcommittee responsible for completing the tasks and activities outlined in the project plan. In this case, the subcommittee file folder would be similar, but would contain documentation pertinent to the proceedings of the subcommittee meetings.

One further note about subcommittee meetings. The subcommittee meeting coordinator or system conversion committee member will develop a list of issues for presentation to the every-other-week system conversion committee meeting. In this way key issues requiring discussion or decisions are brought to the attention of the conversion committee and acted upon.

Most system conversions are not well documented. Adherence to the steps and recommendations for an organized conversion file will be extremely helpful to an organization that plans growth based upon acquisition and/or mergers. Considering that much work goes into any system conversion, it would very beneficial to the organization that the information is not lost and can be reconstructed when the next opportunity presents itself.

ASSIGNMENT OF RESPONSIBILITY TO COMMITTEE MEMBERS

At the beginning of the system conversion process, the system conversion coordinator should define the responsibility of the committee members. Committee members not only participate in the system conversion committee meeting, but their most important role is to coordinate the completion of conversion tasks and activities. Committee members are responsible for executing the project plan through a subcommittee of staff members. These staff members may be formal staff employees reporting directly to the committee member or on a matrix basis. Committee members must understand the importance of their role as well as the need to organize and manage the subcommittee in an effective and consistent manner.

To that end each committee member must develop, in conjunction with the system conversion committee meeting, a schedule of subcommittee meetings. These meetings identify the tasks to be completed, affix responsibility, and discuss task execution progress. Subcommittee meetings pull together the people who complete the tasks and assess status, issues, and concerns. Employees completing the tasks will likely have additional smaller sessions with programmers and other system-related personnel either with the existing processor, in-house staff, and/or the acquired bank's data processor. In all cases it must be understood and recognized that the actual work occurs at the subcommittee level. Based upon the results attained, this information is then reported to the system conversion committee meeting level.

SUMMARY

The purpose of this chapter is to provide a detailed discussion of the preparation necessary for the system conversion process. Before the actual conversion can commence, preparation is necessary to develop the communication mechanisms, structure, processes, and documentation necessary to guide the system conversion. Preparation can aid greatly in ensuring that the process is identified, defined, and organized before the system conversion begins. To that end the basic timeline completion process was outlined. Timelines define the key categories of activities of the system conversion process and therefore are essential for plotting the path of the system conversion, to ensure that it is completed within the time parameters originally established. The timeline template can be used to plot key activities, the time required for completion, and to arrange them relative to each other. The timeline template is used to prepare "what if" scenarios before the actual cutover date is determined. By developing this document, various calendar dates can be input to determine starting dates and feasibility of dates. Critical path charts (CPM) are additional project management tools that are instrumental in understanding the relationship of tasks to one another and to identify tasks critical to the process and subsequent cutover. A tool of this sort can help to plan the tasks and map the tasks that have relationships so as to ensure all are identified.

The kickoff meeting is the event that is the formal start of the system conversion process. To ensure a good kickoff, care must be taken to develop an effective agenda and to ensure that the appropriate participants attend the meeting. In this regard, several necessary steps were identified for preparing for the kickoff meeting. These included (1) developing a list of attendees; (2) determining the date, time, and place of the meeting; (3) developing the meeting memo and agenda; and (4) conducting the kickoff meeting. The agenda should include the following elements: (1) introductory remarks; (2) introductions; (3) CEO and conversion sponsor remarks; (4) review of timeline and targets; (5) review of meeting schedule, format, and process; (6) distribution of project plan and discussion of roles of committee and subcommittee members; (7) question and answer period; (8) conversion meeting beginning and assignment of tasks; and (9) adjournment and scheduling of the next meeting.

After the process has formally been kicked off, ongoing system conversion meetings will be conducted on a regular basis. To ensure these meetings are effective, it is necessary to develop a complete schedule for the entire term of the system conversion, as well as standing agendas and meeting minutes. The agenda for system conversion committee meetings can be a standing agenda rather than newly developed for each meeting. It is important that a routine be established for the conversion committee meeting so that time is not wasted and to ensure that all key elements are addressed as required. Minutes are the record of what transpired at the system conversion meeting. Minutes do not have to be verbatim recordings of everything said but rather an abridged document consisting of (1) promises of action with dates, (2) problems requiring completion with dates and individuals responsible, (3) items requiring decisions from a higher body, and (4) open issues where no resolution is immediately available and which require further discussion and research. The conversion committee meeting flow should be succinct, making the most effective use of time. As a result, the agenda of the meeting should be followed closely to ensure that nothing is omitted. Executive communications was also outlined emphasizing that summary level reporting be directed to an executive committee or governing body for the bank. Summary reporting should be limited to one or two pages, at maximum, and provide an overview of conversion progress. In addition, deferral to the executive committee will occur throughout the conversion process for key pricing, product, and customer communication issues. These items must be directed on a timely basis to this group to ensure that effective decision making occur so as not to delay the system conversion process and jeopardize the cutover date. This may require system conversion coordinator initiation and coordination to ensure timely decisions. Other forms of communication may include referring difficult and troublesome issues to senior managers. These types of communication require tact and diplomacy and must be effectively identified by the system conversion coordinator to ensure prompt resolution.

Work papers and document storage is an important housekeeping issue for any system conversion process. So much information is generated during the system conversion that it must not only be captured and stored for referral, but must be organized for quick and easy access. For this reason recommendations are outlined identifying key sections of the conversion file that should be standard during any conversion process. Conversion work papers should consist of timelines, project plans, minutes, agendas/outstanding issues, executive summaries and decisions, and memos and other related documents. Last, the roles and responsibilities of the committee members are highlighted focusing on members' dual role as conversion committee participant and subcommittee coordinator for the execution of tasks and activities.

This chapter guides the reader and/or system conversion coordinator toward the preparation of the documents, and their flow and process, which are instrumental in designing an effective system conversion.

## CHAPTER 4

System Conversion Data Gathering

OVERVIEW

Once preparation for the system conversion process has been defined and outlined, the system conversion committee can begin to prepare for the tasks and activities that must be completed. This preparation is the start of the system conversion process. This chapter identifies the preparatory items that must initially be determined so that work can be completed according to the information obtained. They will consist, generally, of the various documents, policies, procedures, and other related information needed early in the process so that activities can begin.

This chapter presents a number of preparation tasks and emphasizes the importance and need for developing the information identified below.

1. Site visits and the development of floor plans.
2. Data gathering of basic application system parameters and settings, and assessment of differences between the acquiring and acquired organizations.

3. Financial information comparisons and changes.
4. Duplicate account number listings and analysis.
5. Delivery and flow of work mechanisms.
6. Forms gathering and analysis, internal and external.
7. System security (access) needs and planning.
8. Courier schedules and workflow delivery receipt, and timing.
9. Gathering and review of existing policies and procedures, requiring change.
10. Gathering of existing system and third party contracts and relationships.
11. New location cutoffs and hours of operation.

The focus of this chapter is to identify and discuss those aspects of the system conversion that require preparation or gathering, in advance, to enable those involved in the system conversion to react and address the issues. As will be seen many of the key areas require advance work and time, and for this reason are begun immediately. In this way they do not delay the subsequent start and/or cutover of the system conversion.

SITE VISITS AND DEVELOPMENT OF FLOOR PLANS

As discussed briefly earlier in the timeline template, site visits must commence as early as possible in the system conversion process because of a need to understand the existing technical environment at the newly acquired bank. As indicated in Chapter 3 in the timeline template, site visits should begin approximately 28 weeks prior to cutover. The site visit is a vital ingredient in the process and must be conducted without fail in the case of an acquired financial institution. The site visit should be well organized so that the most can be made of the visit and everything necessary learned or accomplished. When the visit is not structured or organized, vital information may be omitted or overlooked. Some form of checklist must be developed, in advance, that can be filled in by the appropriate systems professionals as they visit the site. An example of a recommended site checklist is shown in Figure 13.

A well-organized checklist should include each area that is important in the process:

1. Type of telephone system.
2. Voice network (whether it exists or not).
3. Data communications network, hardware (analog or digital), and circuits.
4. ATM hardware, network affiliation, and connectivity (remote, lobby, drive up).
5. Current data processor (outsourced or in-house) and hardware, CRTs, and application systems provided.
6. Remote check processing, item capture, and bulk file (in-house or outsourced) contract and/or hardware/software.
7. Cabling. Type of data cabling that exists (or not) within the branches.
8. Type of personal computers. Whether local area networks exist and the type of file servers and other equipment used.
9. Type of teller system (microcomputer based or CRT) and software used.
10. Type of printers, printing (host and LAN).

In order to complete the site survey checklist, it is necessary to contact the appropriate professional in the acquired location who can answer many of the questions posed in the checklist as easily and as nondisruptively as possible. Obviously, the checklist is key to the ease with which information can be captured. This document can and should

F I G U R E 13

Site Survey Checklist

A. MAINFRAME	Page 1

1. Type of service:

                                                        Check one

    a. Service bureau: _____

    b. Facilities management: _____

    c. In-house: _____

2. If service bureau or facilities management:

    Name/address of provider: _____

                                      _____

                                      _____

    Contract expiration: _____

    (Attach contract)

3. If in-house:

    Type/model of mainframe: _____

    Approximate book value: _____

    Date purchased: _____

    Years remaining for depreciation: _____

    Software used (Name and version):

    1. Deposits: _____

    2. Loans: _____

    3. General ledger: _____

| COMPLETED BY: | DATE: | |

FIGURE 13 *(Continued)*

B. CHECK PROCESSING/POD/BULK FILE	Page 2

1. Type of service:

   Check one

   a. In-house _____

   b. Outsourced _____

2. If in-house:

   Type of equipment:

Category	Quantity	Make/Model/Vendor	Age	Book Value
CPU				
Reader/Sorter				
Printer(s)				
Other				

   Back up site location: _____

   _____

   _____

3. If outsourced:

   Name/address of provider: _____

   _____

   Contract expiration date: _____

   (Attach contract)

4. Clearing Agent(s):

ORGANIZATION	LOCATION	DEADLINE

F I G U R E 13 *(Continued)*

B. CHECK PROCESSING/POD/BULK FILE *(Continued)*	**Page 3**

5. Local clearing house affiliation:

   Participation: Yes   _____

                           No   _____

   Name/participants: _____

                           _____

                           _____

6. Approximate monthly item capture volume: _____

7. Courier runs:

BRANCH/LOCATION	PICK-UP/DELIVERY TIMES

8. Proof:

                           Check one

   a. Centralized   _____
   b. Decentralized   _____

   Proof machine equipment:

MAKE/MODEL	QUANTITY	VENDOR

COMPLETED BY:		DATE:	

F I G U R E 13 *(Continued)*

C. ATMs					Page 4

1. ATM card issuer: Yes _____

No _____

2. If yes, type/location/quantity of ATMs:

ATM LOCATION	MAKE/MODEL	REMOTE	LOBBY	DRIVE-UP	WALK-UP

3. Network affiliation: _____
    a. Local/regional: _____
    b. National: _____
    c. Other: _____

4. Number of cardholders: _____

5. Processor (Driver): _____

_____

Contract expiration: _____

COMPLETED BY:		DATE:	

F I G U R E 13 *(Continued)*

D. MICROCOMPUTERS/LANs		**Page 5**

1. Branches networked (Local area network)?:   Yes

                                                        No

If yes:

a. Type of LAN topology: _____

_____

b. Network operating system and version: _____

_____

c. Network equipment:

FILE SERVER HARDWARE	QUANTITY	MANUFACTURER

TAPE BACK UP SYSTEM	QUANTITY	MANUFACTURER

NETWORK COMPONENTS	QUANTITY	MANUFACTURER
UPS		
CAU		
MAU		
LAMs		

2. Networked workstations:

HARDWARE TYPE	QUANTITY	MANUFACTURER

F I G U R E 13 *(Continued)*

D. MICROCOMPUTERS/LANs *(Continued)*			Page 6

3. Printers:

PRINTER TYPE	QUANTITY	NETWKD.	MANUFACTURER

4. Network software:

　a. Operating systems/versions: _____

　　_____

　　_____

　b. Standard network software: _____

　　_____

　　_____

　c. Platform system: _____

　　_____

　　_____

　d. Electronic mail system: _____

　　_____

　　_____

　e. Specialized software: _____

　　_____

　　_____

COMPLETED BY:	DATE:	

F I G U R E 13 *(Continued)*

E. **Teller Systems**	Page 7

1. PC based system?:
   Yes _____
   No _____

2. If yes:
   a. Hardware: _____
   _____
   _____

   b. Software:
       Name/version: _____
       Vendor: _____

   c. Printers:

TYPE	QUANTITY	MANUFACTURER
Screen printers		
Passbook		
Validators		
Other		

3. If no:
   CRT Hardware:
       Type: _____
       Manufacturer: _____
       Controller model/type: _____

4. Number of teller stations:

Location	Stations	Location	Stations	Location	Stations

COMPLETED BY:	**DATE:**

F I G U R E   13 *(Continued)*

F. NETWORK (DATA COMMUNICATIONS)	Page 8

1. Type of network in use:

                                                              Check One

   a. Analog multidrop/point-to-point: _____

   b. Digital point-to-point (proprietary): _____

   c. Digital frame relay (proprietary):   _____

   d. Digital frame relay (public):   _____

   e. Microwave: _____

   f. Satellite: _____

2. Front end processor:

   Yes: _____

   No: _____

   If yes:

      Make/model: _____

      Age: _____

3. Hardware:

	TYPE	QUANTITY
1. Modems:	_____	_____
2. CSU/DSU:	_____	_____
3. Routers:	_____	_____

(Attach Copy of Diagram)

4. Number of circuits:

   a. Analog multidrop: _____

   b. 56 kbps circuits: _____

   c. T-1 circuits: _____

COMPLETED BY:	DATE:	

F I G U R E 13 *(Continued)*

G. NETWORK (VOICE COMMUNICATIONS)	Page 9

1. Type of network in use:

    Check One

    a. Proprietary (tie lines):   _____

    b. Public telephone network   _____

2. If proprietary:

    Type of circuits: _____

    Quantity: _____

| COMPLETED BY: | DATE: | |

F I G U R E 13 *(Continued)*

H. TELEPHONE	Page 10

1. Proprietary system?:

   Yes _____

   No _____

   If yes:

   Vendor name: _____

   _____

   Make/model: _____

   _____

   No. of PBXs: _____

   _____

2. Local phone company:

   Name: _____

   _____

   _____

3. Voice mail user:

   Yes _____

   No _____

   If yes:

   Voice mail system: _____

   No. of systems: _____

4. ACD user:

   Yes _____

   No _____

F I G U R E 13 *(Continued)*

H. **TELEPHONE** *(Continued)*	**Page 11**

4. IVR system:

    Yes   _____

    No   _____

    If yes:

          System provider: _____

           _____

           _____

          Location of unit(s):   _____

           _____

          Monthly call volume: _____

    800 service for access:

    Yes   _____

    No   _____

5. Cable:

    Provider: _____

     _____

     _____

    Type cabling used: _____

     _____

6. Long distance carrier:

    Name/location: _____

     _____

     _____

    Contract term/expiration: _____

     _____

F I G U R E 13 *(Concluded)*

H. TELEPHONE *(Concluded)*	**Page 12**

7. Type of telephone sets: _____

_____

8. Attach lists:

CHECK INDICATING ATTACHED

   a. MB lines, by location: _____

   b. Copies of station reviews _____

   c. Copy of data circuit bills: _____

   d. List of alarm circuits: _____

9. OPX circuits:

LOCATION	FROM	TO

COMPLETED BY:	**DATE:**

become a part of the permanent record and work papers of the system conversion, maintained by the system conversion coordinator.

DATA GATHERING OF BASIC APPLICATION SYSTEM PARAMETERS

The purpose of this preliminary review is to understand the environment of the acquired organization. Not every financial institution has the same products, pricing, and service charge routines as the acquiring bank. For this reason before any system-related conversions begin, it is highly beneficial to gather comparative information. Comparative information is most efficiently developed and identified by building comparative matrices. The information gathered will greatly assist not only the system conversion effort and programming requirements, but, more important the decisions that must be made by the executive group of the acquiring financial institution for any changes or for grandfathering products and services currently in existence.

To accomplish this data gathering, the system conversion coordinator should charge the appropriate system conversion committee members with the responsibility for developing this information. The individuals involved include the marketing/communication representative as well as the operational managers responsible for the products that are sold to customers (i.e., loans, deposits, cash management, etc.). Matrices should be developed to capture and arrange this information so that decisions can be made and/or understood. This will be particularly helpful in a merger. Mergers can be when there is an ownership relationship as in a holding company situation or net new acquisitions that will be merged into the acquiring institution's environment. For any merger/acquisition the following matrices and documents should be developed and become part of the working papers of the system conversion, to be retained by the system conversion coordinator.

1. Service charge matrix.
2. Product pricing matrix.
3. Product and feature comparative matrix.

Service Charge Matrix

Every bank charges customers for various ancillary services provided. These service charges include safe deposit box, stop payment charges, overdraft fees, balance inquiry fees, money orders/official check fees, travellers checks, wire transfers, and so forth. Such fees are very important to determine in order to understand where differences exist between the two entities. If significant change is to be made, effective customer communications are needed to pave the way for new customers. The service charge matrix requires identification of all areas of service charges that exist for both the acquiring and acquired financial institutions (or institutions to be merged).

The document, once prepared, will serve as the basis of communication to the executive committee for service charge decisions on whether global changes will be made or to assess the degree of difference and understand the type of communications necessary to the bank's clients. An example of a service charge matrix that can be used is illustrated in Figure 14. As with all documentation the service charge matrix becomes a part of the documentation and working papers in the system conversion coordinator's conversion file. This document should be prepared as soon as practical, as it is a basis for establishing the programming parameters of the converted systems.

Product Pricing Matrix

Product pricing matrices are twofold, developed for both retail and commercial products. Depending on the institution, other product offerings such as cash management products should also be included. As with the service charge

F I G U R E 14

Service Charge Matrix

	PER-ITEM FEES	
SERVICE CHARGE	ACQUIRING BANK	ACQUISITION
1. Overdraft/NSF fees:		
– Per item		
– Maximum daily charges		
2. Stop payments		
3. Official checks:		
– Cashier checks		
– Certified checks		
– Money orders		
4. Wire transfers:		
– Inbound		
– Outbound		
5. Balance inquiries		
6. ATM fees:		
– New card		
– Annual fee		
– On-us transaction fee		
– Foreign transaction fee		
– Replacement card		
7. Safe deposit box:		
-2×5		
-3×5		
-5×5		
-2×10		
-3×10		
-5×10		
-10×10		
8. Check printing upcharge %		
9. Research charges		

matrix, the differences in product pricing and products offered must be determined. Both of these are extremely important and must be uncovered, as once the system conversion occurs, there will be one product offering list and, very likely, one product pricing list. At the very least, the basic parameters must be similar, as this will be instrumental in making the system conversion either simple or complex in terms of programming. Complexities in product offerings, service charges, and pricing can cause considerable difficulties not only in planning and performing the system conversion but can also create great difficulty in managing after the conversion. This is manifested in application system balancing and reconciliation to general ledger accounts.

As stated previously, product pricing must be determined for both depository and loan products. Another breakdown will be between retail and commercial offerings. Pricing will consist of interest rates paid on deposits as well as interest rates charged on loans. Interest rates alone require the analysis of interest rate plans currently in the database of the mainframe system. This requires gathering information from the acquired bank's data processor (database). Advance knowledge of this information enables the acquiring institution to analyze and make the decisions necessary for going forward. This will involve executive committee involvement. Other areas of pricing include minimum balance charges, and/or transaction fees for deposit accounts.

Again these fees and interest rates should be arranged in a retail and commercial product matrix. Examples of these matrices are illustrated in Figures 15 and 16. This information must be obtained through conversation with the appropriate product managers or other appropriate personnel in the acquired financial institution. As shown in the examples, a column is included that allows for the determined surviving pricing and product listing. This will ultimately be completed from information and feedback provided by the bank's executive committee.

F I G U R E   15

Retail Product and Pricing Matrix

RETAIL PRODUCT	PRICING	
	ACQUIRING BANK	ACQUISITION
Savings		
– Minimum balance required		
– Min. balance charge per quarter		
DDA		
– Minimum balance required		
– Min. balance charge per quarter		
– Per item fee		
NOW		
– Minimum balance required		
– Min. balance charge per quarter		
– Per item fee		
Super NOW		
– Minimum balance required		
– Min. balance charge per quarter		
– Per item fee		
Money Market		
– Minimum balance required		
– Min. balance charge per quarter		
– Per item fee		

F I G U R E 16

Commercial Product and Pricing Matrix

| | PRICING | |
COMMERCIAL PRODUCT	ACQUIRING BANK	ACQUISITION
Commercial checking		
– Minimum balance required		
– Monthly maintenance fee		
– Analysis (yes/no)		
– Earning credit		
– Charge per deposit		
– No. of items free		
– ACH per item		
– No. of ACH items free		
– Charge per item paid		
– Overdraft charge (Avg. coll. bal.)		
Other charges		
– Daily overdraft fee		
– Number of days grace		
– Charge-back fee		
– Check stop payment		
– Telephone transfers		
– Balance inquiry		
– Photocopy of original check		
– Account printout		
– Copy of statement		
– Film copy of check/dep. ticket		
– Money orders		
– Cashiers checks		
– Foreign drafts		
– Domestic—outgoing wires		
– Domestic—incoming wires		

Product and Feature Comparative Matrix

The product and feature matrix differs from the pricing matrix in that this chart displays products and features for understanding and evaluation. The purpose of this document is to show, side by side, the bank's existing products with products currently offered by the newly acquired organization. In this way the detailed features of each product can be compared, side by side, to determine whether the products mirror one another or require some alteration. This will greatly assist in planning for customer communications as well as for the system conversion process. The acquired financial institution may have different names for existing products that have identical features. In this regard once the system conversion occurs the transition will be to a "like" account rather than having to build a totally separate product.

Once this document, an example of which is illustrated in Figure 17, identifies differences that may exist between products, a decision will need to be made by the executive management group on whether the product is discontinued and all existing accounts grandfathered or whether the bank should elect to open a new product. In either case it is important that a solid understanding exists about the differences, as the result will be direct customer impact.

FINANCIAL INFORMATION COMPARISON AND CHANGES

Financial information for a system conversion involves the general ledger, chart of accounts, and the parameters that drive the assignment of costs to responsible departments. Much the same as the product pricing and features comparisons, it must be clear how the acquired financial institution accounts for information. Although the detailed mapping of accounts and the like occurs during implementation, preliminary data gathering can begin the process. This involves not only systems but procedures and policies as well. In

F I G U R E 17

Product Feature Comparative Matrix

	FEATURE COMPARISON	
PRODUCT	ACQUIRING BANK	ACQUISITION
1. Checking (DDA)		
– Interest bearing		
– Free checks		
– Service charges		
2. Money Market		
– No. withdr. per/mo.		
– Checks available		
3. Credit card		
– Annual fee		
– Rate		
– Transaction charge		
– Points earned		
– Home equity		
4. Club account		
– Trav. checks		
– Cashiers checks		

general, the type of information required under the financial caption includes:

- Chart of accounts.
- Reporting package.
- Cost center accounting.
- Product costing and profitability accounting.
- General ledger interfaces.

Chart of Accounts

The chart of accounts represents the population of general ledger accounts open and available for use on the bank's system. This includes all account names and numbers. Each account is used for specific expenses and costs incurred by the organization, and are accumulated into a trial balance and ultimately the financial statements of the bank. When the acquiring bank is planning to merge information from the acquired financial institution, it is important that costs and expenses carry over to the appropriate accounts in the surviving general ledger. To assist in this process, a detailed listing of the acquired bank's chart of accounts should be requested as soon as possible to compare with the existing bank's. All differences should be noted and decisions made as to which accounts will map to which standard bank account. An example of a bank's chart of accounts is contained in Figure 18. The example shows a comparison matrix that can easily be set up to compare the accounts from the two entities. Such comparison will provide advance understanding of how significant the differences are and how much work will be required.

Reporting Package

The reporting package reflects the financial institution's financial statements (balance sheet and income statement). As with the chart of account this document should be requested early in the process, once again to assess the differences,

F I G U R E 18

Chart of Accounts Comparative Matrix

ACQUIRING BANK ACCOUNTS	TO BE USED	ACQUISITION BANK ACCOUNTS	TO BE USED
Assets:			
– Accounts rec.			
– Notes rec.			
– Cash			
– Reserve account			
– Investments			
– Fed funds sold			
– Loans and disc.			
Liabilities:			
– Deposits			

knowledge of which is required to merge the data. Although most reporting packages are relatively standard there will be various nuances, unique to the acquired bank, which will require some discussion and decisions. An example of a typical reporting package is shown in Figure 19.

Cost Center Accounting

Every bank handles cost center accounting differently. Some have elaborate systems developed with many cost centers, whereas others have relatively small systems with few cost centers. Again, if the financial institution uses the host for cost center accounting, basic information should be obtained early to assess how the system is set up and operated.

Cost center or responsibility accounting involves the establishment of unique cost centers for accounting for expenses and revenues generated by the bank. When a financial institution is acquired, the existing cost center system contains a wealth of information, in history of the past year, by detail within specific departments or responsibility centers. This is a very important system for the bank as it provides the channeling of cost information to the areas where managers are accountable and responsible for their use. If the acquiring bank also has a cost or responsibility accounting system, then it is necessary that preliminary comparisons be made to understand where differences lie. Ultimately the goal is to convert existing cost center information to the appropriate responsibility center once the banks are merged. This requires care and attention, particularly if considerable differences exist. In any event obtaining examples of the present reporting package will facilitate greater understandings, which will permit timely action.

Product Costing and Profitability Accounting

Not all organizations have product profitability systems. However in the event that the acquiring bank and acquiree bank both have existing systems of this sort, special han-

F I G U R E 19

Reporting Package

REPORTING PACKAGE—FIRST NATIONAL BANK, AS OF:	12/31/95
ASSETS:	
Cash and due from banks	
Funds sold and other short term investments	
Securities available for sale	
Investment securities held to maturity	
Loans, net of unearned discount	
Reserve for loan losses	
NET LOANS	
Foreclosed real estate	
Goodwill	
All other intangible assets	
Premises	
TOTAL ASSETS	
LIABILITIES AND STOCKHOLDERS' EQUITY	
LIABILITIES:	
Noninterest-bearing deposits	
Interest-bearing deposits	
TOTAL DEPOSITS	
Funds purchase and repurchase agreements	
Other short-term borrowings	
TOTAL LIABILITIES	
Stockholder equity	
Net unrealized losses on securities	
TOTAL STOCKHOLDERS' EQUITY	
TOTAL LIABILITIES AND STOCKHOLDERS' EQUITY	

dling and information gathering must result. Anyone who has developed, or who works with, a unit costing or product profitability system knows and can appreciate the amount of detail that goes into making the system work. In addition to the detail, a number of procedural issues must be adhered to to ensure a common and effective allocation methodology. In short, systems such as this are very sensitive and require attention, otherwise the data could become compromised. When an acquisition occurs, the acquired bank's system must be understood prior to the conversion. In particular, the conversion committee must obtain the procedures as well as the details that form the foundation of the system to understand how costs are assigned. During the conversion all information will be transferred to the acquiring bank's system, which makes the process consistent. However, the goal is to not corrupt the data. This can be accomplished by advance understanding and analysis. When this occurs, the system conversion coordinator will understand in advance how information must be mapped to ensure a smooth transition.

General Ledger Interfaces

The last, but certainly not least important, of the financial issues is general ledger interfaces. Interfaces to the general ledger are vital to the smooth processing of information once it has been converted. These interfaces will likely be established already, and therefore should simply remain intact as the conversion occurs. Most mainframe system conversions provide considerable time and place emphasis on these types of issues, as fundamental to the process. In mergers, however, care must be taken to understanding the interfaces already established in order to be prepared to make modifications, based upon the new needs of the organization. The general ledger interfaces will usually operate with standard application systems, and therefore require a trained eye when analyzing.

During mergers and acquisitions, there are always surprises and differences that were not readily visible at the outset. These differences must be accounted for in a standard fashion in the new entity and therefore must be effectively converted. It is recommended that nothing be taken for granted. When the conversion has occurred, the acid test of whether everything was effectively addressed will be apparent after balancing accounts immediately following the cutover. Without a firm understanding of the interfaces and what went into the conversion, there is a strong possibility that if balancing problems are experienced, they may take some time to resolve. This is undesirable, especially at a time when the bank is most vulnerable, the week of cutover.

The financial accounting area of the bank is an integral part of the conversion process and therefore is vital to a successful conversion. Preliminary data gathering will aid the bank tremendously in planning the changes or transition that is about to occur. Since all of the information processed by the bank must flow through accounting and finance, the integrity of the financial statements is a critical element in the system conversion process.

DUPLICATE ACCOUNT NUMBER LISTING AND ANALYSIS

At the beginning of the system conversion process for a merger and/or acquisition, one of the most important types of information needed is the duplicate account number listing. Duplicate account analysis is a comparison of account numbers from the merger which will indicate whether or not duplication occurs. In many ways the success or problems experienced in the system conversion process will result from the work conducted using the duplicate account list. To proceed it is necessary to acquire a tape of the duplicate numbers from the data processor of the bank being acquired. The tape, once obtained, can be run against the existing file of data on the system to which the acquisition bank will be converted. This matching of account numbers will highlight where duplication exists so that changes can be made.

Duplicate account runs should be done as far in advance as possible. For this reason the task is placed in the preparatory phases or data-gathering stage of the system conversion. In addition, producing the tape will require time on the part of the data processor of the acquired financial institution, as well as time for the acquiring bank's data producer to generate the run. When the list is produced, the conversion committee, particularly the loan and deposit committee members and subcommittees, should be involved to assess where differences exist and develop preliminary plans to address these issues. Duplicate account listings are extremely important because of the customer impact which is involved. Duplicate accounts are not only irritants to customers, but can erode confidence in the bank, particularly at a time when a major transition is taking place, and cause the loss of a number of customers.

DELIVERY AND FLOW OF WORK

The delivery and flow of work involve the movement of paper and documents, forms and the like from one department to another. Additionally, work flow entails procedures for handling the normal duties of the bank, post conversion. In a bank acquisition or merger, these two items are very important. When two organizations are combined, the flow of work previously conducted will change, most dramatically at the organization recently acquired. In addition, other procedural changes will occur at the time of transition, usually because the acquisition sizable enough to require new dimensions in operations to support a larger entity. This could be manifested in an increase in staff or a total change in the location where support is provided. Work flow and delivery require time to consider the obstacles as well as the current process, given the addition of a new entity.

At the start of the system conversion, sound preparation involves a clear understanding of the existing environment as well as knowledge of how the newly acquired bank processes its work. This process should begin as early as possible. Work flow and procedures should never be taken lightly. A sufficient amount of time and the devotion of the right individuals will go a long way toward making sure that all duties are properly and effectively carried out at cutover. When work flow and procedures are not adequately addressed or are given little time for understanding, errors and disruption will likely result. This would be most inopportune for the organization. Whenever a conversion, acquisition, and/or merger occurs, customers are very sensitive to the level and quality of service they receive. In some cases, their fears are unfounded, still, they are bracing themselves for the worst or simply being especially sensitive to the service they receive. Even in the best cases when service has not been eroded, the bank can expect more than the average number of phone calls as a precautionary measure taken by the customers.

To prepare effectively for the transition that will take place, it is necessary to develop a plan for analyzing workflows and understanding where change will take place. In most acquisition/merger situations the following areas will be affected:

1. Item processing and capture.
2. Bookkeeping/statement preparation.
3. Deposit operations.
4. Loan operations and processing.
5. Finance and accounting.
6. Human resources.
7. Credit administration/operations.
8. Information systems/data processing.
9. Teller.
10. Sales.

11. Building and maintenance.

12. Customer service.

13. Purchasing.

Work flow analysis is not merely analyzing procedures. What is important is to understand the flow of work to back-office or support areas, particularly to the ones identified above. It is very beneficial, at this stage, to map out a flow chart of the current process of handling work for both the acquiring and the acquiree banks. By developing the flow charts of activities and comparing them, side by side, it can be readily determined where differences lie and what must be done. With a newly acquired bank or even the consolidation of operational functions, it is necessary to understand how work will flow from one point to another. This will not happen by itself and must be clearly determined, otherwise considerable problems can occur once the newly combined entity begins to function. Additionally, the acquiring bank may learn during this process that the existing work flow and procedures will not be effective for processing work for the combined entity. In this case, the bank may decide that it is prudent to revamp procedures and develop new ones. When this occurs, another element of change is added to the change already occurring as a result of the acquisition. The following material outlines the areas to consider for mapping work flows within each of the operational/administrative areas previously identified.

Item Processing and Capture

In the existing organization checks follow a particular path leading to proof, sorting, capture, transmission to the host, and preparation of a cash letter. In this regard work originates at the branches and must be physically moved from one point to another. This typically is accomplished using couriers. And so, items to consider include the cutoff times of the acquired financial institution, how to get the work to the location providing proof encoding, how to get the en-coded items to the location of sorting, capture, and transmis-sion. In each case the existing bank must integrate the newly acquired bank into the current process or set up a new one.

Bookkeeping/Statement Preparation

Does the existing organization provide this service today or is it outsourced? When the organizations finally convert, it is probable that all work stored and captured will be forwarded to a central site for preparation of statements. Although the acquired organization will not likely perform this service in the future, the current statement preparation and bookkeep-ing area must understand the increased volumes it will assume as well as any changes to statement cycles or special handling that may occur.

This could involve the receipt of statements for prepara-tion at times when they have never been received before. In short an understanding of the changes that will occur must be mapped out physically in order to be adequately prepared.

Deposit Operations

In some financial institutions, deposit operations may be combined with the bookkeeping department. However, in other cases they are separate. Areas for consideration include how the work generated by the sales force is input, research of work, verification, report generation and distribution, stop-payment handling and other back-office areas. In each case, how work will flow from the new entity to the central-ized area must be identified and documented.

Loan Operations and Processing

The same issues as in deposit operations must be investi-gated and analyzed. Loan operations produce loan docu-mentation, maintain files, notes, and records, and perform input of customer payments and other changes to the loan systems. Some organizations also may have centralized underwriting and may use software packages or artificial intelligence to assist in the decision making process.

Finance and Accounting

This area of the bank will be involved in a wide array of conversion-related issues. For the purposes of work flow and procedures, the newly acquired entity will present challenges not only in accounting for information but also for balancing and reconciling either new accounts or growth to existing accounts. Changes will occur for the new entity in processing general ledger tickets, what they look like, when are they prepared, what information is required, and where they go. If this flow of information is not well accounted for when the cutover occurs, problems will surface in the balancing and reconciling function—as rejects, open items, and out-of-balance conditions. Finance also must develop the flow of work for accounts payable and handling vendor invoices. The acquired entity will likely have a number of other relationships, some of which will be terminated, but others of which will continue.

Human Resources

Human resources, obviously, will be involved in a number of ways. Aside from the analysis of staff complement and disposition relative to reductions from eliminating redundant functions, this department must understand and account for how new hires, recruiting, and resignations/dismissals will be handled. Again, because a separate entity has been acquired, how these services will be provided to the branch must be mapped out and understood. There most certainly will be training issues that must be addressed; also paperwork and the flow of such paperwork need to be mapped out in advance. This is important for payroll information, especially considering that payroll is usually processed through systems other than what are found on the mainframe. As regards to recruitment and benefits, will there be local branches for human resource administration or will this be handled centrally? A number of other issues will be unique to the organization; however, these are a few that require understanding and planning for the combined entity.

Credit Administration and Operations

Credit is generally centralized within most financial institutions. Because of the growth in acquisitions, however, and the physical proximity of the acquired locations, some decentralization may occur. In any case, credit must be considered when an entity is acquired. How will credit files be handled? How will they be moved from one location to another? If the bank uses credit analysts, how will sales people request information for statement spreading, credit analyses, and the like?

Collections may be a part of the credit division or under loan operations. For the most part, collection concerns will be handled in the actual system programming and conversion and should not present issues out of the ordinary. If, on the other hand, the acquired bank has a credit card operation not found at the acquiring institution, this must be taken into account when planning departmental needs and transitions.

Information Systems/Data Processing

If the acquiring bank has an in-house information systems department, the same issues must be addressed as in any other operating department. Because of end-user computing, the new site most likely will require an on-site local area network administrator or support individual. Additionally, as new equipment (computers, software, and peripherals) is needed, how does the request flow through delivery and installation from and to the new organization? This division must explore the flow of requests for purchases, telephone and on-site support, installation assistance, and general day-to-day issue handling.

Tellers

Tellers at the new entity need to know how balancing information will flow—to whom and when. In addition, the flow of daily work to couriers and cutoff times must be established. In this circumstance, there most likely will be some form of change from what the acquiree bank is used to. The acquiring bank may need to re-evaluate its entire cutoff structure given the size of the acquisition, physical proximity to the item capture and proof locations, and customer expectations. The new teller system will require different procedures as well as flows of information to the acquisition bank. These, too, must be mapped out in advance for the changes to proceed smoothly.

Sales

Along with the other departments presented, sales too must be considered. Personal bankers and commercial lenders at the new entity process information in various ways. Since sales is the closest to the customer base, extra care should be devoted to understanding the flow of its work. In many cases the sales staff may not be turned over during the conversion transition. Therefore, the flow or delivery of work they are used to will most likely change and so must be documented and understood. Without an adequate understanding of how the current flow compares with the flow of work at the acquired institution, sales staff will revert to their previous procedures, which in turn could cause considerable disruption and negative impact on the customer. From start to finish, the sales area of the bank is critical for work flow analysis and understanding.

Building and Maintenance

At the newly acquired organization the physical structure, environment, and facility was most likely maintained by a local individual. In many cases this will change. When this occurs, what structure or flow exists to handle a building problem, such as electricity, heat, air conditioning, or other environmental or physical issues? This sometimes is easily overlooked, the assumption being that the individual who used to manage these concerns will continue to do so. Unfortunately, when reductions in staff occur during the conversion, such individuals may no longer be employed. The result could be disruption or inadequate working environments. In short, this area must not be overlooked.

Customer Service

Depending on the organization, customer service may be handled locally (at the site), regionally, or centrally. When a new entity is acquired, it is extremely important to map out the flow of customer calls into the newly combined entity to ensure that adequate support and service are readily accessible. This, of course, may not only require adjustments to the existing phone system and flow, but will also involve understanding what to communicate to customers as to where to call. This may also be addressed within the programming area of the system conversion because of the involvement of customer statements and notices that direct a customer to call a particular number to obtain service. As with sales, extra care should be taken to understand how service is provided now and how it will be provided in the future. Inadequate attention and/or poor documentation can result in customer dissatisfaction and turnover. When the actual cutover occurs, the number of customer calls will likely increase. If service is inadequately provided, the problem will be attributed to the conversion/merger and erode customer confidence. The bank may lose customers as a result.

One should not overlook any type of electronic answering equipment that may be used, such as voice response units. These must be reprogrammed to serve the newly acquired customers, and the way calls flow through the bank customer service system will change.

Purchasing

Purchasing of supplies and equipment in the new structure will be different from what the acquired institution is used to. Furthermore, the proper venue for the flow of requisitions must be determined, such as whether it should be via telephone or through a form. If it is to be a form, how will it be sent, retrieved, and handled from the new entity. Although this may appear to be less significant than other areas, if purchasing is not well structured and mapped, individuals will have difficulty performing their jobs without adequate tools and supplies. If employees cannot get basic supplies such as key forms or paper, it will make them less productive and less effective in servicing customers and performing their duties. Again, careful attention to analyzing and understanding work flows is of major importance.

As emphasized in the last several pages, work flow and procedural analysis is a major aspect of the system conversion process. Systems will be programmed and converted in conjunction with the mainframe (host) processes; however, each time a system is changed there is a corresponding change in procedures and work flow. Particularly in the case of mergers, where organizations as well as functions are coming together, flow cannot and will not be the same as before. This must be understood in advance. The organizations that plan effectively for this by following the steps outlined, documenting current and future flows, will be ahead of the game and will improve the chances of a successful transition 100-fold. There may be other areas of the bank, not mentioned, that require this type of attention and consideration. These should also be considered and documented.

Since every financial institution is different, different nuances will occur. However, there will always be a core set of functions that must be addressed to be successful. The ideas presented will pave the way for developing and mapping the kind of information needed for successful conversions.

FORMS GATHERING AND ANALYSIS (INTERNAL AND EXTERNAL)

Although technology is rapidly moving in the direction of a "paperless" society, this has yet to happen for financial institutions. Banks, today, are as much paper intensive as they have ever been. This is evident in the wide array of documents and forms used to perform the day-to-day functions of the banks. When a merger or acquisition is about to take place, a primary area requiring advance preparation and data gathering is that of forms. There is no question that the acquired bank will need to change its forms to process data correctly and without rejection, and also to account for letterhead changes, MICR, and other legal and electronic requirements.

The compilation of forms for an acquisition bank requires time and organization. The sheer volume of forms is extensive and requires someone who understands the financial institution and the specific areas within to ensure that all forms, notices, and written material are accounted for. Because forms must be printed, lead time is required so that appropriate supplies can be obtained in time for distribution, training, and implementation. For this reason the accumulation of forms falls under the preparatory stage of data gathering. Advance data gathering must begin as soon as practical because, depending on the size of the organization being acquired, large volumes of different forms may be in use. Not only must plans be developed to increase current stock levels of forms for the conversion, but new forms, unique to the organization, may be required. An example of this is account brochures. The acquired entity may have a unique product that the acquiring bank would like to retain. In this regard, new brochures and information need to be developed in the appropriate quantities. In addition to understanding the types of forms, contact must be made with the vendors supplying the forms to inform them of the transition.

To adequately prepare for the conversion and begin the data gathering process, one must know where to look for the many different forms. To facilitate this process, a checklist of forms is presented in Figure 20. The checklist can be used as a guide in any system conversion involving an acquisition and/or merger, the most common forms of which are listed in the figure. Forms are identified by functional area, and should follow the chart outlined below. These forms, again, are the most frequently used items and should be physically obtained from the new entity. As the forms are obtained, they should be checked off the list and placed in an envelope labeled with the designated department. Separating forms into categories helps to simplify the process and identify the needs for the newly acquired entity.

Department	Forms Used
Human resources	– New hire applications
	– Employee change forms
	– Benefit forms
Teller	– Cash in and out tickets
	– Deposit slips
	– Withdrawal slips
	– Official checks
	– Money orders
	– Travellers checks
Sales (personal bankers)	– Signature cards
	– New account applications
	– General ledger tickets
	– Passbooks
	– Certificates of deposit
Sales (commercial)	– Corporate resolutions
	– Notes

Department	Forms Used
	– Documentation checklists
	– Personal financial statements
Finance	– General ledger debit tickets
	– General ledger credit tickets
Operations	– Stop payment forms
	– Input forms/documents
	– Transaction forms
	– Loan applications

It is important to begin gathering forms as soon as possible because of the lead times for ordering and also because of the decision process that is involved for any changes that may occur. Never assume that all forms will carry over and simply use existing forms of the acquiring financial institution. Changes will inevitably be required because a number of areas are receiving considerable attention and scrutiny. When this occurs, often-postponed alterations and/or deletions are highlighted thus need changing. Seldom do bank personnel have the time to review forms and documents on an ongoing basis to make the necessary changes. The attention afforded by the system conversion will likely trigger evaluation and scrutiny.

SYSTEM SECURITY (ACCESS) NEEDS AND PLANNING

System security predominantly involves user access to the mainframe system and the various applications for inquiry and/or maintenance. The reason for this is that in an acquisition or merger-originated conversion, system security plays a key role in access to and utilization of the mainframe application systems once the cutover occurs. Although this is the major reason for security consideration, there will also likely be a number of other security access needs that merit advance scrutiny at this stage. These include local area net-

F I G U R E 20

Forms Gathering Checklist

TYPE OF FORM	RETRIEVED		COMPARISON TO EXISTING FORMS		
	Attached	Not Attached	Retain	Change	Not Needed
HUMAN RESOURCES					
1. New hire applications					
2. Employee change forms					
3. Benefit forms					
TELLER					
1. Cash in and out tickets					
2. Deposit slips					
3. Withdrawal slips					
4. Official checks					
5. Money orders					
6. Travellers checks					
SALES					
1. Corporate resolutions					
2. Notes					
3. Documentation checklists					
4. Personal financial statements					

work access to software and files and voice mail user security among others.

User security must be planned in advance and information obtained in order to effectively plan for the transition. To accomplish this data must be gathered regarding the available users who require access to key systems, what functions they perform, and what their position is in the organization. Similar to the other areas within this section, preparing information related to security needs can easily be accomplished using a data gathering document. An example of this type of information gathering and tracking is illustrated in Figure 21. The following provides additional explanations and information regarding each area of security to be analyzed.

Mainframe Security Access

Mainframe security involves the user security assigned to individual employees for access to key application systems. These include access to the deposit, loan, and general ledger systems, to name a few. Employees of the newly acquired organization require access to these systems to perform their day-to-day duties. Functions and tasks these individuals perform are inquiry access, maintenance of accounts, opening and closing accounts, and other related functions. For each user not only must a specific user identification be established, but security level access must also be assigned to each user. This will include specific transaction types that would typically be used.

Mainframe security requires timing and precision in the process of development. The reason for this is that the acquired institution's employees will likely begin using the new security on the day of system conversion cutover, not before. In this scenario the system conversion coordinator, through the security committee member, needs to prepare and test the new security codes prior to assignment and use. The testing will probably take place during the weekend of

F I G U R E 21

Security Analysis and Planning Form

NAME	POSITION	LOCATION	TYPE OF SECURITY (please record user ID assigned)			
			Mainframe	LAN	Long Dist.	E-Mail

conversion. In the planning for this area, the initial goal is to identify those new employees who will require access to the mainframe system. This can be learned only by communicating with the managers who will be responsible in the new physical entities. The information obtained should be recorded on the planning document. The important information includes

- Name.
- Position.
- Location.
- Application systems used.
- Transaction/functions performed within each.

Once this information is captured, it will easily facilitate the assignment and development of security in a timely and efficient manner. Use of the planning document provides additional time in which to develop such information in advance.

Local Area Network Access

If the acquiring bank has local area networks and an end user computing system, the new facilities acquired will be retrofitted to mirror those of the larger organization. When this occurs, employees need to be identified according to the local area network (file server) where their work is performed. Similar to mainframe security access, this consists of the establishment of a user ID for each employee. This can be further complicated if the acquiring institution has a wide area network. In this scenario, users will also require identification at remote file servers where file and software access is needed.

Local area network user security is usually assigned by the local area network administrators or central LAN administration. The security for LAN access requires some of the same information as indicated under the mainframe

system conversion; however, additional items must be determined. The base information required is

- Name.
- Location.
- Workstation and equipment identification.
- Application software to be shared.

The same information-gathering document can be used as in
the mainframe security document. The user would merely
fill in the appropriate lines and boxes. Again, as with mainframe security, it is important to ascertain who and what
information access will be required in advance, in order to
allow as much time for development as possible as well as to
build an effective document for ongoing referral as part of
the workpapers.

Voice Mail Security Access

Voice mail, if available, requires the establishment of a user
ID for accessing voice mail messages. Whether or not the
acquiring bank has voice mail, a new mailbox and security
access will need to be developed. Similar to the other areas,
information should be attained in advance during data gathering to develop a document with all pertinent information
to establish this voice access. The document in Figure 21 will
suffice for capturing the data needed for this.

Long Distance Codes

Some banks have systems in which long distance dialing is
tracked using long distance codes. Many long distance car-
riers have programs by which detailed information can be
captured about the calling patterns (and costs) of individuals making long distance calls. This adds another dimension to the security access system for new employees of the
acquired entity, which will require setup on the long dis-

tance carrier's system. Obviously, the financial institution will have individuals dedicated to this system for assignment. However, during this phase of data gathering, as much information as possible should be obtained. The document in Figure 21 is all encompassing in that it effectively provides a means of capturing and storing which individuals require what long distance access, and to what degree. In this way, proactive efforts are made to provide codes only to those individuals who require such access. Advance data gathering and planning assist in communicating information when it is needed to avoid disruption at the time of cutover, when focus and attention to other issues are most important.

Electronic Mail Access

If the financial institution uses an electronic mail system, the issues previously discussed would apply here as well. System security for sending and accessing electronic mail messages need to be defined and input when the time is appropriate. This may be before the actual cutover, in which case advance planning of security access will aid greatly in ensuring proper setup and access to data. E-mail may not be used broadly within the bank. For this reason care must be taken in determining who should have access to the system and what features they should have access to.

The security form provides a workable document for the development and assignment of the required levels of security for all systems. To the extent that the information is well organized, it will go a long way toward ensuring uninterrupted access to information and functions on the systems the bank uses. When this step is overlooked or poorly handled, tremendous disruption can occur once the cutover occurs. If tellers cannot access the host, customer dissatisfaction will result from long lines and delays. The goal of any system conversion is to provide for as smooth a transition as possible at system cutover, so that it is as transparent as possible to the customer. Delays or errors in permitting users access to systems will impair their ability to service customers and do their job.

COURIER SCHEDULES, WORKFLOW DELIVERY AND RECEIPT, AND TIMING

All financial institutions are paper intensive. That is, paper in the form of checks, deposits, general ledger tickets, and other documents flow through the system. In particular, checks taken at the various branches must be physically moved to central sites for preparation for proof encoding, cash letter development, sorting, capture, and transmission to the host. To accomplish this, a network of bank couriers must exist to shuttle the documents and work to their respective destinations. For checks, this not only involves the physical move of the document but also when it occurs and how frequently are of paramount importance. When checks are sent to a central processing location, timing and frequency are important to ensure that the work ultimately is combined in the form of a cash letter, which is sent to the bank's clearing agent.

Because an acquisition always involves the addition of a new location or branch structure, a new courier schedule or addition to the existing one must occur. As with all information, this requires time and care so that the financial institution does not miss opportunities for receiving credit for deposits because of delays in courier schedules resulting in late cash letters. Furthermore, during the information gathering phase, it is necessary to determine what cutoffs the acquired institution has used in the past. Some banks have early cutoffs, in order to process work effectively, to meet certain deadlines. Others offer same day credit and hold all work until the end of the day. In either scenario, the acquiring bank must look at what will prevail in terms of cutoffs, and evaluate the locations of the acquired branches to determine what will be needed in terms of couriers and schedules to move and process work at the required times. This can be organized, gathered, and documented in a form as shown in Figure 22. This document organizes the data and guides the preparer to seek specific information when meeting with bank personnel. Documentation in this form ensures that nothing is missed and that the information becomes a permanent part of the workpapers for future referral.

When evaluating the cutoff scenarios of the existing bank and determining the impact of the changes, one should always consider the monetary impact on the combined entity as well as the impact on the customer. In some cases, depending on the location of the acquisition, it may be too costly to transport work more frequently to and from a distant site. The trade-off is the amount of work generated from the branch, at given intervals, which dictates whether it is cost effective to schedule more courier runs to ensure that work flows steadily to the central processing site. Again, depending on the location and number of branches acquired, the acquiring institution may want to reconsider its entire pickup and delivery schedule. If so, advance preparation and understanding of information obtained is an absolute must.

In addition to checks, couriers typically move other types of work to and from branches, such as reports, documents, and interoffice mail. During the data-gathering phase, attempts should be made to develop a list of all documents, forms, and communications that are picked up and delivered for the bank being acquired, as well as for the acquiring financial institution. Comparing transported items will reveal what must be accounted for, or accommodations that must be made, for uninterrupted functioning. This is easily accomplished by developing a side-by-side chart that will quickly reveal deficiencies or additions that will be required upon conversion. A simple chart, as shown in Figure 23 will aid the user in recording currently transported documents as well as documents not accounted for. By performing analyses of this sort, decisions can be made regarding the type of information needed within the new branches.

F I G U R E 22

Branch Cutoff and Courier Schedule

BRANCH	CUTOFF TIME	COURIER PICK UP/DELIVERY TIMES				
		Monday	Tuesday	Wednesday	Thursday	Friday

FIGURE 23

Document Flow Comparison Chart

Acquiring Bank Type of Document	Continue (yes/no)	Bank Acquired Type of Document	Continue (yes/no)

This analysis serves to ensure that important information, documents, or forms are not missed, which may be relied upon even after cutoff. Mergers and acquisitions cause considerable change, both in procedural flow and personnel and it is relatively easy to lose sight of a particular document needed by an employee.

Unfortunately, this is often not known until the week of cutover, or even after in some cases. The result can be lost opportunities, errors, or other detrimental events that may not be immediately apparent. It is well worth the time to understand the information flow and make conscious decisions as to the disposition of the information. In this way proactive rather than reactive actions will prevail, which is highly desirable in any system conversion.

GATHERING AND REVIEW OF EXISTING POLICIES AND PROCEDURES

Policies and procedures in a system conversion are a given. That is, the acquiring financial institution already has these established. Unfortunately, during any system conversion, based upon the unique needs of the acquired bank, these policies and procedures may change. Furthermore, the surviving employees at the acquired financial institution are not familiar with the policies and procedures of the new group. One must always consider first, the size, location, distribution network, and clientele of the acquiree. It is entirely possible that the acquired institution is equal in size to the acquiring bank or has a much larger and diverse distribution network. In this case, many existing policies and procedures will undergo alteration to accommodate the needs of the newly combined entity. Employees of both the acquired and the acquiring financial institution need to understand these policies and procedures.

As with everything in a system conversion, information must be gathered to understand in advance the depth and volume of policies and procedures that exist in the acquiring institution. Procedures and policies should also be gathered from the organization recently acquired. This will enable a comparison of differences to aid in future development and communication. The first step, then, is to simply locate and compile copies of existing key procedures and policies from both institutions. The next step is to list and review, side by side, the type of policies and procedures in existence to determine which are new to each organization. This can be accomplished by simply setting up two columns and identifying the policies and procedures by name as shown below.

Acquiring Bank	Acquiree Bank
1. *Policies:*	
Credit policy	Credit policy
Fixed-asset policy	Fixed-asset policy
Expense policy	Expense policy
End-User policy	None —————
None —————	Overdraft policy
2. *Procedures:*	
Stop-payment handling	Stop-payment handling
Computer equipment purchase	None —————
Supplies purchase	Supplies purchase

The above abbreviated example provides a glimpse of what this type of analysis might look like. It is an effective way to document existing policies and procedures (or lack thereof) within the organization. Where there is a deficiency, a decision must be made as to what to do and a note added indicating that communication and training are required for the individuals in the organization where the policy or procedure will be introduced. Additionally, this process documents the population of policies and procedures, providing the system conversion representative with a basic array of those that will be important in the combined entity. From this list, actual policies and procedures can be compared and contrasted, in particular for nuances in the acquired institu-

tion that must be added to existing procedures of the acquiring financial institution. Never assume that all policies and
procedures will be carried over fully intact to the combined
entity. There will always be some form of change.

Finally, once the list is developed, compared, and differences noted, an outline of the new list of procedures and policies should be developed. These are policies and procedures
that will prevail at the conversion and for which training and
communication will be required. The list should take the
form of a table of contents for a *Policies and Procedures Guide*,
which can be shared with the combined group and will provide the steps and rules by which the combined entity will
operate. This is important in the conversion process. It is from
this information that surviving employees of the acquired institution will operate. Therefore, it is important that the information be organized in a format that permits both easy access
and clarity of understanding when used by the employees.
The outline or table of contents should be the first page in the
Policies and Procedures Guide. Establishing this type of manual
will enhance the organization's ability to acquire and/or
merge financial institutions into the bank in the future much
more efficiently and with minimal effort. A goal of this publication is to identify and document the process that can be
used over and over for future acquisitions so that less time is
required and conversions occur with minimal disruption
and in very predictable time frames. Developing such documentation and adding to it as organizations are acquired will
provide a central repository that everyone can benefit from
when procedures and policies change.

GATHERING EXISTING SYSTEMS AND THIRD-PARTY CONTRACTS AND RELATIONSHIPS

With every acquisition, a new repertoire of relationships and
agreements will exist. Since many of these will not continue
to exist postconversion, information gathering and analysis

are an absolute necessity early in the conversion process. As soon as possible, the system conversion representative should begin to gather and document a list of services provided to the financial institution by third-party vendors, as well as actual agreements and contracts. Normally, an assessment of these is made at the time the bank is considering the purchase of the financial institution, and buyout clauses are typically factored into the consideration offered in the acquisition. Many contracts and relationships require advance notice of termination within specified time periods. These must be known and arrangements made to provide the notifications required in the contracts to the third parties so that they coincide with the actual cutover. In some cases, contractual terms may terminate prior to cutover. When this occurs, there is a time gap between when the service is to be terminated and the conversion or cutover occurs. Obviously, service must continue during this time, so arrangements must be made to go on a month-to-month basis until the conversion occurs. Most third-party vendors are prepared for this and will usually extend a contract monthly until the time of the conversion. Unfortunately, the pricing may not be attractive simply because no leverage exists with the provider that ultimately will be terminated. This is a cost of the conversion and must be viewed as such. The additional cost is generally preferable to having to accelerate a conversion and not provide the time needed to merge the entities in a smooth and uneventful manner. This would most likely occur for the acquired bank's data processor and other significant services provided to the bank. To facilitate information gathering and assessment, a listing of areas in which review should occur to determine the level of coverage and/or service provided is presented below. These will (or might) apply when acquisitions occur.

Potential Area of Coverage or Service Provided
1. Data processing services (outsourced).
2. Outsourced item capture and bulk file.

3. Cash letter clearing agents.
4. Credit card third-party processor.
5. Merchant credit card processor.
6. Data network communications support.
7. Mortgage servicing/processing provider.
8. Vendor equipment purchase relationships:
   - Computer equipment.
   - ATMs.
   - CRTs/controllers.
   - Telephones.
   - Cabling.
   - Alarm systems/security.
9. ATM network affiliation and processing agreements.
10. Courier arrangements/agreements.
11. Maintenance agreements:
    - Software.
    - Computer hardware.
    - Photocopiers and other office equipment.
    - Other areas

The above list is not exhaustive, but provides a checklist of some of the major relationships that exist for a particular financial institution. Each of these agreements must be reviewed to determine the impact of continued processing and/or termination upon conversion. The list should continue to evolve during this process—as new areas are discovered they should be added, with copies of contracts produced and reviewed. During the data-gathering phase, the conversion representative should interview selected individuals to determine relationships that exist, which must be considered during the overall system conversion process. In some cases, as the details of the agreements and contracts are revealed, a decision may need to be made by the executive committee or senior-level executive in the bank. In this case the conversion representative must communicate with the system conversion coordinator during the system conversion meeting or individually to ensure that the issues are raised to the next level for discussion and decision making. This may be the case with major relationships, such as an outsourced data processor, which will require some time and consideration depending on what is required. For other functions a determination must be made as to whether the relationship will continue. If the relationship will not continue because the acquiring bank has other relationships or means of providing the service, then termination letters must be sent to the organizations according to the requirements of the agreements.

With some of the larger or more complex agreements, there will likely be clauses that indicate the disposition of the contract in the event of an acquisition. These should be reviewed by the bank's attorney to ensure that appropriate steps are taken and proper disposition occurs in accordance with the terms.

LOCATION CUTOFFS AND OPERATION HOURS

This may seem an obvious item of information to be gathered, however the need for this information as early in the process as possible is of paramount concern. The hours of operation for the facilities drives a number of other actions that are and will need to be performed. Furthermore, will these hours continue postconversion? In some cases the answer will be that the acquiring bank's hours of operation will prevail. However, this is not necessarily the case. Depending on the size of the acquisition and the clientele, exceptions may be needed, at least for a period of time until the transition is fully accepted. When a conversion occurs, customers typically expect the worst. They invariably are sensitive to even the most minute changes and attribute these to the insensitivity of the acquiring institution. In this regard it behooves the acquiring financial institution to give consideration to the most obvious customer concerns, and make any modifications that can be made, albeit temporarily. Remember, the most sensitive time, from a customer perspective, is when the conversion actually occurs. Customers actually anticipate problems. Because of this, defer as many noticeable changes as possible until the combined entity has established its reputation and provided uninterrupted support and service. Changes can be made at a later date with less negative impact than at the time of conversion.

The noticeable changes referred to include hours of operation and cutoff times. Cutoff times were discussed earlier with regard to courier schedules and workflow. However, it deserves repeating here in that changes to cutoffs can affect more than just courier schedules. If the acquired bank had no cutoffs, and all work was completed at the end of the day with same-day availability to the customer, any change will be to the customer's detriment. In this case, there would be an immediate erosion of service, one that would require disclosure. Cutoffs due to geographical location may be a necessity to get work to a central processing point for the acquiring bank, but the change requires preparation and communication. As stated, the first would be a disclosure communication to customers. Second, procedures for tellers would change if mid-day cutoffs occurred, which in turn would affect teller balancing. This, in turn, would affect the proof encoding schedules and delivery of work to central processing sites. In short, a change of this nature triggers a number of events. Although it may not be avoidable, data gathering and planning must occur in advance to map out the ramifications of such a change.

The hours of operation for the sites also are a consideration. When a bank is acquired, may have different hours of operation than the acquiring bank. This is most apparent to a customer if there is a decrease in the hours of operation. If hours are changed, a number of events will need to be addressed including customer communications, advertising, courier pickups, on-line availability, and others. To address these issues, the system conversion representative involved should prepare a chart of the locations of the newly acquired organization. The chart should show the hours of operation for all areas, as well as cutoffs that currently exist. Such information should also be recorded for all of the acquiring organization's branches. This should all be gathered and documented on a worksheet similar to the one illustrated in Figure 24. As the information is determined, the worksheet should become a part of the conversion workpapers for future reference. In addition, this should be the document that shows all changes that will be made so that they are recorded and documented in one place.

SUMMARY

Data gathering is a very important part of the system conversion process. System conversion projects sometimes have a tendency to blend activities in an effort to meet time deadlines. This invariably causes errors and problems that will arise at inopportune times. A financial institution serious about growth through acquisition and merger must have a well organized and systematic process to incorporate financial institutions efficiently and effectively and plan future combinations. A fundamental part of this is the ability to gather, document, and organize information vital to the conversion process and to act on it.

Data gathering was outlined in a number of vital areas of any acquisition. Site visits and obtaining floor plans was discussed. Early access to the acquired bank is important to assess what technical changes will be required during the conversion process and to outline the basic floor plan of the facilities. This is necessary so that data and voice cabling can be planned to retrofit the branches to the technology currently employed by the acquiring bank. This will include microcomputers and local area networks, telephone connectivity, voice networks, network printing, electronic mail

F I G U R E 24

Current Hours of Operation/Cutoff Existing and Change Schedule

ACQUIRING BANK				BANK ACQUIRED			
Location	Lobby Hrs.	Drive-Up Hrs.	Cutoff Time	Location	Lobby Hrs.	Drive-Up Hrs.	Cutoff Time

communication, voice mail, and branch-to-branch communications via a wide area network, if available. The physical site will need to be reviewed to determine where equipment rooms can be set up for PBXs, file servers, modems, and other communication devices. Site visits also provide a cursory examination of existing equipment to determine if advantage can be taken of existing equipment.

Similarities and differences in basic system application parameters are obtained through communication with bank system professionals, operations contacts, and/or walkthroughs. Such items as service charges, product pricing, products, and product features are major issues that require advance information. Information of this type can be gathered by using matrices, which will become part of the system conversion workpapers and basis for decision making and changes. Each of these items requires advance understanding to determine which products will remain or be changed, what service charges will prevail, and general product pricing parameters. These areas are vital for system programming and preparation for the actual cutover, as well as customer communication.

Financial information is required to determine differences between the two institutions. Changes to reporting packages, charts of accounts, cost centers, to name a few, must be understood and considered in advance to determine how the system will be developed for the conversion. Duplicate accounts are one of the earliest areas for data gathering because of the pervasive impact on the customer base resulting from duplication. Duplicate account listings are usually obtained from the data processor for the acquired entity and must be analyzed to decide what changes are to be made. These areas have immediate impact on the customer, and the degree of care taken can make the difference between a successful and unsuccessful conversion.

Work flow and delivery are often less well planned aspects of system conversions. Work flows will invariably change when a conversion occurs, simply because new locations are added and work must flow to and from the new branches according to new schedules. In this regard, changes to procedures will occur and will affect a number of bank employees. Work should be flowcharted, to the extent possible, analyzing delivery sequences and tasks performed at each level. This provides graphic documentation of what currently transpires and facilitates understanding and changes as they need to occur.

Forms and other documents used by the bank were also discussed. Financial institutions are very form-intensive. Physical walkthroughs are important to pick up examples of all forms and documents used by the acquired entity. These are necessary to understand what documents require change. Comparison to forms currently used helps to ensure or determine whether the forms can be used as is or whether alteration should occur. A newly acquired entity may need additional forms not currently used by the acquiring bank. This can only be determined by physically gathering such documents. Finally, forms, especially, must be analyzed very early in the conversion process because lead times must be taken into consideration for replenishing stock of existing forms or for ordering new forms in sufficient quantities for the combined entity.

Access to bank systems for completing daily work and servicing customers requires the change of mainframe security access codes, as well as a number of other security accesses. Today financial institutions are very technology driven, which requires an array of security codes to access the various systems in the bank. This will certainly involve mainframe access; however local area networks, voice mail, electronic mail, and other areas are typically also involved. As with forms, advance documentation of individuals and requirements helps the planning of the security system for uninterrupted access to information at the time of conversion.

Courier schedules, hours of bank operation, and cutoff times must also be determined to establish the flow of work and time of day for processing. These involve analysis of the location of the branches and their proximity to the processing centers of the acquiring bank. The cutoffs and courier schedules depend upon one another and have an impact on the customer base. Care should be taken when making changes so that minimal negative impact is experienced by the customer during the system conversion. To plan effectively for this, it is important that this information be gathered, documented, and analyzed in advance for decision making.

The last areas discussed were the gathering of existing policies and procedures and third-party contracts and agreements. Policies and procedures will change at least for the acquired bank's employees and perhaps for the acquiring institution as well. Policies and procedures must be analyzed in advance to determine what they are and what they provide. This helps to establish which should continue, which should be added, and which should be abandoned. The data gathering should form the rudiments of a table of contents for a *Policies and Procedures Guide,* which can be used to communicate to new employees what will occur at the time of conversion and beyond. Contracts and third-party arrangements, on the other hand, must be located and reviewed as soon as possible to determine the various requirements for continued service, termination of service, or provision of temporary month-to-month service in the event that the contract expires prior to system cutover. These documents are extremely important to understand in advance so that opportunities are not missed and disruption of service does not occur.

In general, data gathering is a process that pulls together information and prepares the system conversion team for analyzing and answering the questions about the changes that must be made. Time must be incorporated into the system conversion process as early as possible to permit the site surveys, data gathering, walkthrough, and flowcharting for activities, as this will form the basis for making required changes for operating the combined postconversion bank.

## CHAPTER 5

Nonsystem Considerations

OVERVIEW

Nonsystem considerations are involved in any system conversion process. Any acquisition requires attention to and consideration of areas that will be affected by the business combination. These areas, although not involved in the technical aspects of the conversion (mainframe conversion and programming, end-user computing, network, etc.), must nevertheless be considered in the overall system conversion process, because they affect personnel and what occurs within the branches. Some of these areas have already been noted either in the development of the timeline template and/or in the data gathering and preparation phase of the system conversion. The purpose of this chapter is to devote attention to the specific issues and rationale surrounding these areas and to provide more background as to what must be considered in the system conversion process.

In this chapter the following topics are discussed:

1. Human resource concerns relative to the new bank and staffing the branches.

2. Management and coordination of physical facilities added to the bank.
3. Types of communication, internal and external, required during the conversion process.
4. Training needs and timing relative to new and existing employees.

Each of the above areas requires further consideration because of their importance in the system conversion.

The conversion process should take into account these areas and seriously focus on the efforts required to complete the tasks and activities required of each. The previous chapter discussed how information for these should be gathered. As this information is obtained, actions will in some cases be required that may not relate directly to the system conversion process itself but nevertheless must be considered. In this regard each deserves discussion to provide the reader with a complete picture of issues that will probably need to be considered in any conversion, particularly those resulting from acquisitions.

HUMAN RESOURCES ISSUES AND CONCERNS

It is obvious that in an acquisition and/or merger there will be human resource considerations. In addition, however, staff issues result from other types of system conversions as well, for example, when a new software and hardware system is installed. This usually has been purchased to improve productivity and will likely affect the number and deployment of existing staff. To this degree the human resource department should be part of the process, at least in a peripheral fashion.

Human resource considerations are important in any merger or acquisition. When a new organization is acquired, there most likely will be an impact on back-office operations, as the acquiring bank generally will want to centralize functions as much as possible. This will result in a reduction in the staff of the acquired financial institution. Most acquisitions require this type of change—it is a necessary part of the transition to meet the financial objectives of the acquisition. In other words, organizations are purchased in the belief that the acquiring bank can run the new organization more efficiently with its existing operational structure. As a result, the human resource department must become involved relatively early in the process for a number of reasons. Early involvement is important because the complement of staff at the acquired bank must be determined with profiles of the employees. In this process, key individuals must be identified who are important, if not critical, to the system conversion process. They must be retained, if possible, throughout the system conversion process. This may require bonuses to induce employees to remain during this period. It will also involve effective communication and counseling in advance to ensure that this occurs. In this regard, human resources fulfills a critical role to help ensure the success of the system conversion.

The system conversion requires the involvement of key operational people at the acquired financial institution. The reason is that they have the knowledge and understanding of how existing systems have been set up and any special arrangements that have been made to accommodate customer needs. This will be difficult to understand unless the originators of these nuances are available for consultation. The availability of key employees will aid greatly in minimizing work and providing a deeper understanding of the issues involved. During the conversion process, key employees in specific areas need to be identified to become a part of the system conversion committee. Each system conversion committee member on the acquiring bank conversion team must have a counterpart on the acquired bank side. These are the individuals who will guide the conversion through the special setups and issues unique to that bank. The areas of the acquired bank that must be represented on the system conversion committee should be as follows:

1. Deposit operations.
2. Loan operations.
3. ATM/EFT operations.
4. Information systems (telephone, network and end-user computing).
5. Item processing.
6. General ledger and finance.

This is the minimum number of employees, considered critical to the process, who must participate in the system conversion process from the organization being acquired. Human resources should make every effort to identify these individuals and retain them through the conversion, if possible.

The role that human resources plays is to identify the critical players and work with them as soon as possible to understand their disposition before any of them becomes disgruntled and leaves the bank. In addition to retaining key employees needed in the conversion, human resources should be involved in identifying the employees who will remain, in all areas, postconversion. This includes names and profiles of employees in sales as well as operational and support areas. The complete list of employees obtained should be documented such that notations can be made about employees who will remain and those who will not because of centralization or absorption of the function (i.e., support or operations, generally). This will greatly assist in determining which players the system conversion coordinator can select from to add to the committee meeting. This should be done as early in the process as possible. In this way the employees who will likely remain will be easier to determine. To facilitate this process, Figure 25 provides a chart for gathering employee information on any acquisition and to organize the data for use.

Human resources must play an active role in understanding the employee environment and situation at the acquired bank. This, as stated, must be addressed as quickly as

F I G U R E 25

Employee Disposition Chart

DEPARTMENT	EMPLOYEE NAME	BRANCH/ LOCATION	RETENTION STATUS		CRITICAL FOR PROCESS	
			RETAIN	NOT RETAIN	YES	NO

possible to be certain that proper communications occur with the present employees, as their status will be in a state of transition. More communications and discussion is always better than less. When human resources does not communicate with the new employees, staff members will become concerned. This could result in premature resignations, particularly of key people important to the process. Attention to these issues improves the chance for a successful system conversion.

PHYSICAL FACILITIES AND BUILDING MAINTENANCE

When an organization is acquired, in more cases than not, bank buildings and physical facilities are part of the transaction. This adds to the base of bank buildings of the acquiring financial institution. In the conversion process, plans must be made for managing and maintaining the physical facilities. Care must be taken so that if employees leave during the conversion, buildings and equipment continue to be maintained. An example of this is preventative maintenance in key areas such as backup generators or uninterruptable power supplies. Maintenance personnel typically perform a variety of routine functions. These include checking and monitoring various aspects of the building to ensure uninterrupted service. This is often taken for granted. When staff begin to leave, and they will, when a conversion is announced or is in process, important jobs may no longer be done. In many cases this is not a concern as functions will be absorbed by the maintenance staff of the acquiring bank, but when the duty is of a critical nature, problems can occur. Many key systems are maintained by power generators and UPS systems. These systems require ongoing maintenance and servicing. When they are not maintained, the absence of this monitoring will be felt when a minor disaster occurs, such as a power outage. Once this happens plans are usually put in place to correct the situation, but by that time the damage may be done.

Building and equipment maintenance should be planned for in advance as an area requiring attention during conversion. Physical facilities may not require the conversion or reprogramming of mainframe systems, but the devices that access these programs are housed within the physical facilities and depend on power and other devices for their ongoing availability. Many times these areas are not considered until a negative event occurs or until well after the conversion process is completed. It is the recommendation of the author that this area be an important part of the conversion, although not directly related to system programming, training, and other changes. The acquiring bank should focus early on these physical needs, since once the business combination is announced, other concerns may cause them to be overlooked. To facilitate this understanding and attention, the system conversion representative should begin to develop a list of critical building aspects. It requires some data gathering to determine how things are maintained, what protection exists, and who currently provides the service. Once this is understood, plans can be made for contingency measures and points of vulnerability can be identified. Figure 26 illustrates a worksheet of key physical areas, support needs, and impact on systems within the bank. The example focuses on a number of key areas that should be considered whenever a new building is acquired. The system conversion representative should use the worksheet to ensure that primary areas are covered, which will help tremendously in avoiding negative occurrences at inopportune times. It is important to remember that any area left unattended has the potential of "rearing up" at a time when it can create considerable disruption, such as at cutover. When problems arise at or around the cutover, considerable disruption can occur at a time when attention is focused on other, more critical, issues such as the system conversion itself. The impact, unfortunately, is felt by the customer, when this is not necessary.

F I G U R E 26

Critical Physical Facility Considerations

CRITICAL PHYSICAL AREA	EQUIPMENT TYPE	WHO MAINTAINS	MAINT. FRQCY.	SUPPORT VENDOR
1. UPS systems				
2. Generators				
3. Electrical breakers				

COMMUNICATIONS
(INTERNAL AND EXTERNAL)

Communications is a definite part of the system conversion timeline, even though it may not be directly related to the system aspects of conversion. Communications take many forms, and must all be well planned and coordinated so that they happen at the right time to address the right issues. For these reasons a detailed communication plan must be developed in advance of any system conversion. This type of planning can be very helpful for ongoing acquisitions and mergers that may occur in the future and predominantly follow a particular pattern. In general communications fall within several broad areas:

1. Customer communications.
2. Internal bank employee communications.
3. External third-party communications.

To be effective in the communications listed above, a matrix and plan should be developed for each which identifies the type of communication, form of communication, supporting manager, timing of the communication, and the status. The status of the communication is used for identifying when communications have been completed, or issues that may impede communicating.

Communications should be coordinated by the marketing or public relations officer of the acquiring bank. The plan recommended above should be developed and managed by this individual, who will be a direct participant in the system conversion committee meeting as outlined in Chapter 2. Each broad area of communication should have a separate plan including the categories previously outlined.

Customer Communications

Customer communications are those that are directed to the customer base of the newly acquired bank, as well as to the existing clientele of the acquiring bank. Communication of this sort must be made, and planned for, at various intervals throughout the conversion process. Time will be required to prepare the communications, place orders, and prepare for the distribution of the communications. In Figure 27 a planning chart is displayed that identifies the general areas of customer communications, arranged within the categories previously identified as important for planning and implementation. In general, for most system conversions involving mergers and/or acquisitions, customer communications will consist of:

- Duplicate account notifications (commercial and retail accounts).
- Retail/commercial service charge brochure.
- Customer service phone number changes.
- Wire transfer customer change in ABA# notifications.
- ATM network disclosures and new/renewed letters.
- Notification of change in bank name.
- Notification of change in statement cutoff dates.
- Notification of change in daily cutoff times.
- Notification of conversion week downtime schedule.
- Other miscellaneous communications.

Duplicate account notifications. Duplicate accounts are probably the most important consideration in the system conversion process. As stated in Chapter 4, duplicate accounts must be identified in advance to develop plans for addressing the changes required. There will undoubtedly be duplicates that must be addressed. Duplicate account numbers must be changed. The changes must be communicated to the appropriate customers. The marketing area must prepare letters that identify the new account numbers, the reason for the change, and assurances that the changes are necessary and that no detriment will result for the customer.

Retail and commercial service charge and pricing brochures. When a merger or acquisition occurs, service charges and ac-

F I G U R E 27

Customer Communication Plan

TYPE OF COMMUNICATION	FORM OF COMMUNICATION	SUPPORT MANAGER	TIMING OF DISTR.	STATUS
1. Duplicate account letters				
– deposits				
– loans				
2. Commercial pricing				
3. Service charge brochures				
4. Customer service/other phone numbers				
5. System downtime letters/signs				
6. ATM disclosures				
7. Product disclosures				
8. Bank name change notification				
9. Other signage changes				

count pricing will likely change, especially for the bank being acquired. Changes of this sort must be communicated to the customers as effectively as possible at the most opportune time with respect to the system conversion. Service and pricing information is usually sent to customers on at least an annual basis. The documentation prepared in this scenario requires some form of cover memo to explain to the customer the changes and clarify the reasons for such changes.

Customer service phone number changes. Upon completion of the conversion, customers must know who to call when questions arise regarding their accounts. The clientele will most likely place numerous phone calls immediately following the conversion with a myriad of questions. Whether or not the acquiring bank has a centralized customer service operation is of no consequence; changes will result from the business combination. The acquired bank does not normally answer customer service inquiries. They are usually handled by the acquiring financial institution; therefore, changes in phone numbers must be communicated. This is particularly important for mergers and acquisitions. Customers must know where to call at or around the time of system cutover. Otherwise they may become very concerned about the stability of the organization and may move their accounts elsewhere.

Wire transfer changes. When the conversion occurs, the wire transfer function will continue; however, customer ABA numbers will change. These must be communicated to customers so that wire transfer services can continue unimpeded. Again, advance letters must be sent to the customers. In addition to letters, it is desirable that telephone communications be used as a follow up to draw attention to the letter and ensure that bank clients understand the changes.

ATM network disclosures. Depending on the location of the acquisition, the regional network affiliation of the acquiring bank's customers may require a change. In this situation, much advance communication must occur as well as the renewal of existing customer ATM cards. Furthermore, as customers switch to a new network affiliation, additional letters must be drafted and sent to ensure that the customers understand the changes. In some cases no changes will be required. Even so, there still may be changes to ATM cards, in terms of account numbers and other types of affiliations. Again, advance customer communications greatly assist customers in understanding the changes, and enable customers to continue to use the services of the bank without disruption. A goal of any system conversion for mergers and acquisitions is to ensure just that.

Notification of change in bank name. An obvious communication is to notify the customer of any change in bank name and the timing of this change. This is a good opportunity to assure customers of a smooth and uneventful transition. The acquiring bank should view this as a marketing opportunity, using it to establish confidence and credibility in the new banking organization. When banks are acquired, confidence and credibility are often most affected by the change. The correct type of communication to the customers goes a long way toward ensuring a smoother and more effective transition.

Notification of statement cutoff changes. When banks merge or a new organization is acquired, there is a strong possibility that existing statement cycles will change, at least for the customers of the acquired financial institution. This has obvious and immediate impact on the customer. If a change is required, customers used to receiving statements by a specific date must be told in advance that this will no longer be so. Another point of consideration is that customers who have had their canceled checks sent to them every month may no longer receive them. Some banks totally truncate checks, which means the checks are not returned with their statements. Although their are pros and cons to this, from a customer viewpoint, communication must effectively address this issue.

Notification of change in daily cutoff times. As discussed earlier, due to the physical distance of the newly acquired financial institution, item processing work may not be able to be held until the end of the day prior to pickup for proof and forwarding to the item capture point. If this is the case, and more than one pickup is required, this will likely result in changes in cutoff times for the bank. This can have immediate impact on the customer by way of eroded availability. Certainly, if cutoff changes occur, advance communications must be made in such a way as to convey the logic and compensation involved. In other cases, there may be elimination of cutoff times due to more effective processing and pickup schedules. This too must be communicated, with emphasis on the benefits for the customer.

Notification of conversion weekend downtime. Most system conversions occur over a weekend. During this period there is always a likelihood that some level of service may become impaired. Although efforts are made to avoid this, no guarantees can be made that it won't happen. In this regard it is important that advance communications be made to customers so they are aware of what could occur. Proactive communications are always prudent in that customers appreciate knowing ahead of time what to expect rather than finding out under negative circumstances. In addition, the bank may wish to ask customers for advance forgiveness for problems that may occur. This can be in the form of "pardon our dust" letters or even posters in the bank lobby for customers to see.

There may be other types of communications to customers beyond those indicated above. These must also be made in advance and should be as specific as possible. The more the communications, the better off the combined entity will be in retaining customers. Advance thought and planning in these areas will not guarantee that customers will remain, however, it will certainly make customers more knowledgeable and increase their confidence in the bank.

Internal Employee Bank Communications

Beyond external customer communications, a number of other communications should occur to bank employees throughout the process of system conversion. Every communication made to the bank's customers should also be made to the employees of the bank. In particular, these communications must be made to the sales staff and other employees who have regular customer contact. When system conversions occur, communications within the bank (both acquiring and acquiror banks) are not always made on a regular basis. This, unfortunately, is due to a variety of reasons, but in most cases it is due to time demands and a lack of planning, attention, and preparation of these notices. For this reason it is highly recommended that the marketing or public relations staff develop a plan, similar to the customer communication plan, which will provide some form of newsletter, memo, or verbal communications of the latest events in the system conversion. When the system conversion involves the combination of a number of branches, employees, and customers, it is important that the bank develop some formal method of internal communications. This sends a message to the staff that they are a part of the process and considered important in understanding the events as they occur throughout the system conversion process.

As stated, internal employee communications should, at the very least, include everything communicated to the customer base. This information will in one way or another be needed by the internal users to assist them in performing their functions. Basic communications should be documented in a plan, similar to that of the customer communication plan, as shown in Figure 28. It is precisely this type of discipline that is necessary when planning internal staff communications, otherwise communication will not occur or will not be in a timely manner, causing more confusion and disruption than what they were originally intended to prevent. The types of communications to internal employees during a system conversion involving a merger and/or acquisition include

- Customer communications (as reflected).
- Changes in management/key employees.
- Status of the system conversion and issues.

F I G U R E 28

Internal Employee Communication Plan

INTERNAL COMMUNICATION	INDIVIDUAL RESPONSIBLE FOR COMMUNICATION	TARGET DATE	COMMUNICATION STATUS/ISSUES
1. Customer communication			
2. Changes in management/key employees			
3. Status of system conversion/issues			
4. Changes in products/pricing or features			
5. Department phone number communication			
6. Procedural/policy changes			
7. Name changes and timing			

- Changes in products, pricing and/or features.
- Communication of department phone numbers.
- Procedural/policy changes.
- Name changes and timing.

Customer communications. These are the same communications sent to customers. Internal users should receive exact copies of what is sent to customers in order to adequately prepare them for customer questions, concerns, and problems that may arise. If kept informed, employees are more likely to put forth their best support and service to customers at a challenging time.

Changes in management/key employees. As the system conversion progresses, changes in personnel will inevitably occur. This will consist of changes in management at the new facilities resulting from redundancy of function, reduction in force, or simply employee resignations. When these occur, some form of communication should take place to keep individuals informed of changes in personnel they may have been working with and to identify to whom changes are being made. The most frequent criticism of system conversions by internal employees is a lack of communication and a sense of knowing who still performs what functions. A well-organized system conversion anticipates these issues and does not leave to chance or the grapevine what staff changes have or will occur.

As changes occur, new employees and managers should be introduced to the staff either in a communication newsletter or verbally in periodic meetings.

Status of system conversion process and update. Employees of both the acquiring and acquired financial institutions should be made aware periodically at a meeting of how the system conversion process is progressing. It need not be a detailed meeting similar to the system conversion committee meeting but can be a high-level overview meeting indicating the progress status. Meetings of this sort should communicate to employees whether the planned cutover is on sched-

ule or not and what changes may be taking place along the
way. The more communications that are provided to the
bank at large the better all employees will be able to act in an
informed fashion as they carry out their jobs, whether they
are directly involved in the conversion or not.

Changes in products, pricing, and features. When products
must be changed, grandfathered, or otherwise, not only must
the sales staff be made aware of what and when, but so too
must other staff members. Many staff individuals have
pieces of input or involvement in the products of the bank.
Keeping employees informed of new products on a timely
basis will help them to do a better job. In addition to new
products, pricing and product features will also likely
change, at least for the acquired financial institution. This
type of information is critical to the sales force and other key
operational employees. Service charges may not necessarily
change nor new products be needed; however, understanding that employees other than merely the conversion
committee need to be informed is a positive step toward
successful conversions.

Communication of department phone numbers. Department
phone numbers will change once the conversion is nearing
completion. This is virtually unavoidable. To provide ongoing communication, it is recommended that changes to the
bank's telephone directory be made weekly at least four to
six weeks in advance of the cutover. These changes should
continue, on a frequent basis, following cutover until internal
stability is achieved. If the acquiring bank does not have a
telephone directory, or has one not easily updatable, a special
directory should be developed of key departments and employees. This directory should be arranged on a functional
basis, with the second part of it for employee listings, in
alphabetical order. The functional directory should consist
of an alphabetical listing of key departments, with primary
employees and phone numbers under each. If the organization is relatively small, the functional directory can list all
employees within each department. The second part of the

directory would simply be an alphabetical listing of all employees and their respective phone numbers. The departments that should be included, at a minimum, in the functional directory are

- Information systems.
- Credit administration.
- Marketing.
- Accounting and finance.
- Purchasing.
- Investments.
- Building and maintenance.
- Human resources.
- Deposit operations or bookkeeping.
- Loan operations.
- Customer service.
- Training.
- Compliance.
- Loan documentation.
- Item processing and capture.

There can certainly be more; however, these are the basic departments to include. Telephone directories can make a big difference in the smooth transition of the conversion and foster effective communications.

Procedural/policy changes. Policy and procedures have been mentioned several times as important considerations in any system conversion. Although it is extremely important to understand existing policies and procedures for changes, it is absolutely vital that they be communicated effectively to internal employees. The method of communication can be a challenge, however, to ensure that all appropriate employees are communicated with effectively. In some cases manuals have been developed that identify all primary bank policies and procedures that should be known on a global basis. Although this can be an effective method of communication, people generally are fairly busy during a system conversion process and may not read the manual. Because of this, arrangements should be made to not only deliver the manual to the employees but also to develop a forum to communicate the highlights of the procedural and policy changes. This is an important recommendation because employees often do not read the manual, especially if it is relatively large. A manual is still appropriate, however, since it will be a reference book for future use. However, when the cutover occurs, employees must know and understand any changes that have occurred or will occur.

Name changes and timing. In the preceding section, reference was made to communicating to the customer changes in the bank's name. This is equally as important to the employee. Employees must have a good sense of what changes are transpiring for their bank or place of employment, especially if they are likely to interface with customers. Again, the more communication in this regard, the more knowledgeable the employee base will be.

Employee communications are always acknowledged to be important, but they are seldom accomplished with the precision of other aspects of the system conversion. The difference between effective and ineffective conversions could be how well the staff is informed. Time must be made to ensure that communication occurs on a regular basis, regardless of the effort needed. The benefits of an informed employee base will be a more effective transition.

External/Third-Party Communications

The last area of communications in the system conversion process is the external, third-party world. The external world is that which involves individuals other than direct customers or employees of the bank. Third parties are vendors and other providers of service to the bank, as well as other bodies that should be made aware of changes taking place. Third parties can include outsourced companies, suppliers, providers of computer hardware, maintenance providers, couriers, building and equipment vendors, and others that have relationships on a regular basis. These organizations must be identified and a mailing list developed so that communications can be provided. A second group of third parties includes the Federal Reserve bank, correspondent banks, the American Bankers Association and state associations, and any other organization that needs to know what is occurring during the system conversion process.

The type of communication that third-party organizations require is generally different from that needed by customers and employees of the bank. Generally, the communications will be more detail oriented. Certainly communication of any change in name and address is a must for all third-party organizations. Beyond this, however, some vendors may require more detailed information in order to continue to provide effective service to the bank. To facilitate these communications, the system conversion representative can begin with a listing of all third-party organizations—the address, contact, and type of service provided by the organization as shown in Figure 29. This type of worksheet will help to gather and organize information unique to both the acquiring and acquired institutions. As data is gathered and documented, communications with other members of the bank can determine the level of service provided by such third parties so that the appropriate communication can be drafted and distributed at the proper time. Third parties, unlike customers or employees, are relatively few in number. It is important, however, to document who the third parties are and identify what types of communications they will need. When identifying vendors requiring communications, the conversion representative may not be able to ascertain what type of communication is needed. This will need to be determined from various operational and support contacts who work with the third parties and can easily find out what is required. Once the worksheet is complete, the conversion representative should have the operational contacts identify the format and type of communications form to be sent.

F I G U R E 29

Third-Party Communication Worksheet

THIRD-PARTY RELATIONSHIP NAME	ADDRESS	SERVICE PROVIDED	CONTACT NAME	PHONE NUMBER

TRAINING

The last area of consideration for nonsystem-related functions is training. Training has been discussed throughout this book in a number of ways. Initially training was identified in the development of the timeline template as well as in the preparation phases of the system conversion process. In virtually any system conversion, training must be seriously considered because change will occur. The newly acquired organization will be converting to a new set of procedures, policies, mainframe systems, telephone systems, and other related software systems. As a result, training will be a major consideration throughout the process. Unfortunately, when a bank acquisition occurs, the level of training in today's world must be more extensive than in the past. A number of years ago when a conversion occurred, most of the training involved the mainframe system. For the acquired organization, most of the support and back-office functions would likely have been centralized in the acquiring bank, and therefore would have required less training. The staff remaining at the acquired financial institution would not need as much training because of their manual processes. Today, however, this is no longer true. Most, if not all, financial institutions are computerized. That is, heavy reliance is placed on end-user computing and sophisticated telephone and communication systems to conduct day-to-day business. In this regard the training requirements for the newly acquired entity will be extensive. Because of this, training must be well planned early so that the training demands do not all occur within a short span of time. For training to be effective, adequate time must be allotted between training sessions for practice and absorption before something else is added to the knowledge base. This means careful planning and scheduling of training requirements and sessions.

When an acquisition occurs today, the type of training typically required of the new staff involves a number of areas that are predominant in most banking organizations today. These include

- Telephone system and voice mail.
- Voice network communications.
- Microcomputer basics and standard applications.
- Local area network operation.
- Electronic mail communications.
- Platform and teller software applications.
- Mainframe software application.
- Other peripheral systems (optical, image, etc.).
- Procedural and policy training.

For each area an optimal amount of time is required not only for the actual training but also for allowing an interval between one application and another. In other words, training for the above items is likely to be required for any organization acquired. When this occurs, it cannot simply be scheduled one week after another. This will not permit time for absorption of knowledge and practice, and will create confusion and disruption at the time of cutover. Unfortunately, virtually all of the training areas will be needed at the time of cutover, which adds to the complexity. Definite plans must be made to coordinate training and to establish what intervals will be needed in between.

Based on the requirements for processing of new information, the time needed for acceptable absorption of information for the areas presented should be developed as shown in Figure 30. This planning document identifies the number of weeks prior to cutover in which training should occur and the actual duration of training for each area. This planning document can be used to overlay on the overall timeline to record the actual calendar weeks for each training item. Training, unless planned for, will not adequately be accomplished. If training is inadequate, back-office areas will likely be deluged with work attempting to address rejects and errors due to a lack of understanding. Very early in this

F I G U R E 30

Employee Training Planning Document

TRAINING AREA	DURATION OF TRAINING	WKS. REQ. PRE-CUT	ACTUAL DATE	TRAINER
1. Telephone/voice mail	one-half day	12–5		
2. Voice network	one-half day	12–5		
3. Microcomputers	one day	9		
4. Local area networks	one day	9		
5. Electronic mail	one-half day	7		
6. Platform/teller training	4–5 days	2		
7. Mainframe	one-half day	2		
8. Other	one-quarter day	2		

book the comment was made that the bank cannot shut its doors for a few days to allow for proper training, practice, and testing. When training is rushed or superficial, the work must still get done because customers will not stop. As a result of this, even though employees do the best they can, errors will occur. These errors result in out-of-balance conditions, rejects, and other negative circumstances, which will require additional work on the part of the back office for correction. This has a detrimental impact on the combined bank and can easily elongate the overall conversion timeline. Also, the financial institution cannot capitalize on planned opportunities nor take advantage of future bank combinations until it can control and stabilize the situation.

Telephone System and Voice Mail

The newly acquired organization must be able to communicate with customers and other members of the bank. To do this training for using the telephone handsets and features and to access and record voice mail messages is an absolute must. Today telephone systems can do much more than in the past. Employees must be taught how to conduct three-way or multiple-person teleconferences, transfer of calls, voice mail broadcasts, and a wide array of features that did not exist in the past. Voice mail, especially, is a major communication mechanism, in that messages left by customers and other employees must be accessed regularly. Employees must know how to do this.

Telephone training should be performed first during the conversion process. The reason is that it is not driven by the mainframe system and therefore can be completed early. This is strongly recommended, since communication is critical in the overall system conversion. If it is addressed early, there will be more time to adjust to the new system, which should provide a high level of competence by the time the cutover occurs. Telephone training should be conducted approximately 12 to 15 weeks in advance of the cutover.

Training does not require considerable time. However, to ensure that effective time is devoted to this area, at least three to four hours will likely be needed to impart the knowledge required. With telephones and other areas it is important to consider refresher training at a later date as well. Staff members will grasp the basic functions relatively quickly, and once they begin using the telephone system and voice mail, they will obtain the necessary practice. Unfortunately, most employees do not use the system effectively in terms of the many features it has. Therefore, refresher training at a later date is highly desirable.

Voice Network Communications

Not all organizations have dedicated voice networks. However, with the increase of mergers and acquisitions, more branch networks will exist, crossing telephone LATA (local access transport areas). When this occurs costs will increase. Because of this many organizations set up tie lines or other networks, which can permit ongoing calling without steep costs. To ensure that employees use this training it will be required to ensure that costs are minimized. Training for this can occur in conjunction with the telephone system training, as the network (if available) will be installed at the same time. This training is not intensive and involves an understanding of what code to use when dialing within the group.

Microcomputer Basic and Standard Applications

Microcomputer training will be required when the acquiring bank has an end-user platform system and/or PC-based teller system. If the acquired financial institution is not used to microcomputers, training will be required. Microcomputer training is intensive in that time is required for practicing to ensure proficiency. If the bank relies on platform and/or teller systems that are PC-based, employees must be comfortable with basic microcomputer use before they can learn more sophisticated software. For this reason training is recommended approximately nine weeks in advance of cutover. The reason is that once the new employee is trained on microcomputer basics, six to seven weeks of practice on microcomputers will provide proficiency before new software demands are placed on the users. The duration of the training is generally one day and will require education not only on how to operate a PC but also the basics of the operating system and any standard application software used, such as word processing and spreadsheet.

Local Area Network Operation

Most organizations that deploy large numbers of microcomputers do so in a local area network (LAN) environment. If this is the case, employees must also learn how to log in and use the LAN effectively. This includes how to share files on the server as well as software sharing and network printing. This training should be conducted at the same time as microcomputer training. The reason is that the part of the basic operation of a PC requires logging onto a LAN. It cannot be avoided if this is the present architecture. Nine weeks in advance of cutover provides adequate time for practice prior to the addition of further areas of knowledge.

Electronic Mail Communications

Not all organizations utilize electronic mail (E-mail). If it is used, however, much of the communication will occur using this software and communication methodology. This type of communication, then, must be trained for in advance to allow as much time on the various communications as possible, since this will be instrumental in facilitating communications within the "to be combined" bank.

Because this is another dimension to the use of the computer, training should not occur at the same time as the

LAN and microcomputer basics training. It can, however, occur after at least two weeks, or approximately seven weeks prior to cutover.

Platform and Teller Software Applications

Both platform and teller systems have evolved in banking over the last few years. Both are microcomputer based and require training and understanding of how to use the software systems. Training for each assumes that the employee knows how to use a microcomputer. For this reason basic microcomputer operation occurs much in advance, at nine weeks prior to cutover level. If this occurs within that time span, the employee should be ready to learn a more sophisticated software package. Most platform automation system software packages are extensive, that is, they are large systems used to perform all personal banking functions on-line. Sometimes these systems are called sales support systems, because they are complete sales systems that guide how bankers sell and position products and services to customers. For these reasons training will also be extensive. Training for a system of this sort requires more than one day, perhaps three or four days of training. Such a system cannot be implemented until the cutover to a single mainframe system occurs, so training should be conducted as close to cutover as possible. The recommendation is to conduct this training approximately two weeks in advance of cutover so that individuals will remember what they have learned when the cutover occurs. The same holds true for a PC-based teller system. Although tellers require less training, they too should be trained approximately two weeks in advance. The duration of training for tellers, however, will be approximately one day.

Mainframe Software Application

The mainframe system software requires training for access and understanding of the various transaction codes and aspects of the system. Because this will not be available to users until system cutover, training should occur as close to the cutover as possible. For the sales and teller staff, mainframe use can be incorporated within the platform and teller training, as both systems will likely be integrated. However, for other users who do not rely on the platform or teller system, additional training may be required. Given that the most mainframe access, other than sales or tellers, will be by back-office and support personnel in the acquiring bank, training for this type of access alone would be minimal.

Other Peripheral System Training

Other systems such as optical disk or document imaging sometimes are used by banks. Access to these systems requires training, as employees of the newly acquired financial institution will need to use these systems at the time of cutover if this is how documents and reports are accessed. Optical disks may be used for overdraft or other types of reporting used by bankers on a regular basis. Similar to mainframe training, this education should to occur as close to the cutover as possible, or within one to two weeks of cutover.

Policy and Procedural Training

The last area of training, but certainly not least important, is the policies and procedures, which will change as a result of the business combination. These policies and procedures are those previously drafted to account for the changes in the way work flows and is conducted in the combined bank. As stated, these documents can be put into a reference manual. It is necessary, however, that the key policies and procedures be communicated to the bank's employees so they understand the changes and what to do once the actual system conversion occurs. This training and communication should be conducted approximately one week in advance of the cutover. Again, policies and procedures will in most cases take effect once the conversion occurs. Given all the activities occurring at or around the cutover, employees probably will not remember policy and procedural changes for extended periods. The week before cutover will be hectic, but this is the appropriate time to conduct training for these issues.

There will be a great deal of activity as the conversion progresses toward the cutover. For this reason attention must be placed on planning and organizing how and when training will occur. Again, training is often overlooked or given cursory attention. Today, however, there are so many areas that require training that it is a priority for system conversion.

SUMMARY

Chapter 5 highlighted areas in which systems are not the predominant or driving factor in the conversion process. These areas are, in most ways, integral parts of the conversion process, as they affect a number of concerns in the system conversion. Today bank acquisitions and mergers involve a wide array of functions to ensure a smooth transition. Each of these functions must play a role in the entire process to ensure that nothing is left to chance. If not, the bank runs the risk of eroding customer confidence. Human resources must be involved because of the effect of the conversion on staffing. An important consideration for human resources is to identify key employees within the acquired bank who must be retained throughout the system conversion process. These are employees knowledgeable about the current system setups who will be instrumental in ensuring that the nuances of the previous system are accounted for and adequately transferred or incorporated into the new system. Human resources can play a significant role in helping to ensure that these people remain within the organization until the conversion issues are addressed properly to minimize customer dissatisfaction at cutover.

Physical sites and facilities (buildings) is another area of consideration whenever a bank acquires another financial institution. When an acquisition is announced, maintenance and management of buildings of the acquired financial institution must continue. This can be overlooked if staff members, particularly building and maintenance people, leave the organization. Like many of the nonsystem areas, planning and organization are important for understanding areas that could be left unattended. Backup systems and environmental issues may be overlooked until it is too late. When this occurs, negative consequences could impair the bank's ability to provide products and services to its customers effectively at a time when customers are most sensitive.

The last two areas in the chapter focused on communication and training. Communication and training are major nonsystem functional areas vital to the system conversion process. In both cases planning documents and organization are most important to identify and plan for the work needed to be done throughout the conversion process. Communication and training are both functions that must be conducted throughout the system conversion. Timing is important for completion of these items. In this regard, careful planning must be done to ensure that communications are not only defined but prepared so that they account for the three major categories of communications: (1) customer communications, (2) employee communications, and (3) external communications. Each requires different types of communications that must be clearly identified. This type of advance planning and documentation helps ensure that communications are made in a timely manner. Training also requires precision in scheduling and timing. A variety of training is required whenever a system conversion involves an acquisition or merger. Today training requirements have grown considerably beyond mainframe application systems. With the use of new technological methodologies in banking, the training required has increased substantially. Microcomputers, network utilization, electronic mail, and other types of technologies are now needed for financial institutions to be competitive. This makes the system conversion process more complex and requires greater planning to be effective. Planning is critical because various nonsystem elements must be integrated in the process. Both system and nonsystem elements are important to the overall system conversion. The time spent planning and organizing to determine when and how these should be executed can make the difference between successful or unsuccessful conversions.

Implementation

OVERVIEW

This final chapter is devoted to the last element of the system conversion process, implementation. The previous chapters discussed developing, organizing, preparing, and gathering information for the system conversion. The last step is putting everything together and implementing the various elements leading up to and including the actual conversion weekend and cutover. Chapter 6 presents the following learning objectives, relative to the final phase of the process.

1. Technical installations and activations of microcomputers, telephones, cabling, and platform and teller software.
2. Mainframe conversion requiring product mapping and setup, programming, test reports, and acceptance.
3. Remote processing activation.
4. Security user ID and other technical passwords and applications.

5. Conversion weekend walkthrough planning and occurrence.

6. Conversion week activities.

7. Acceptance.

This chapter is somewhat of a capstone in that it pulls together the various preparatory and data gathering phases into the final act of installation and implementation. This portion of the system conversion process, if organized according to the recommendations outlined in this book, is the culmination of all prior efforts and should be entered into with confidence. Discussion focuses on the issues important and germane to the installation of the elements of system conversion process. The implementation phase of the system conversion is generally separated from the preparatory, training, and communication phases, and so this final chapter is devoted exclusively to the actual implementation of the various elements of the conversion leading to system cutover. An example of the completed timeline is illustrated in Figure 31.

Each section or learning objective identifies, in detail, the issues, concerns, and activities involved in the implementation of that particular aspect of the conversion process.

Technical Installations and Activations

The activation, installation, and implementation of the various technical systems must occur in the sequence presented previously in the timeline template. Because the technical elements require advance preparation and have a major impact on all aspects of the acquisition, the timing of the installations must be coordinated in a staggered fashion throughout the entire system conversion process. For the technical installations the work involved concerns a number of people and occurs simultaneously with other implementation steps. These areas include

Comprehensive System Conversion Timeline (page 1)

#	TASKS	RESPONSIBLE
A	**TELEPHONE SYSTEM**	
1.	Site visit and information gath	Telecommunications Mgr.
2.	Plan telephone/PBX hardware needs	Telecommunications Mgr.
3.	Purchase/order telephone hardware	Telecommunications Mgr.
4.	Installation of the PBX	Vendor
5.	Telephone station reviews	Telecom. Specialist
6.	Telephone handset placement	Vendor
7.	Voice mail ID build/setup	Telecom. Specialist
8.	Activate phone system	Vendor
9.	IVR programming	Telecom. Specialist
10.	Other network programming	Telecom. Specialist
11.	Activate IVR and other systems	Vendor
B	**CABLING**	
1.	Site visit and information gathering	Telecommunications Mgr.
2.	Obtain floor plans of facility	Telecommunications Mgr.
3.	Plan the install of voice/data cabling	Telecommunications Mgr.
4.	Order cabling/approval	Telecommunications Mgr.
5.	Cable installation	Vendor
C	**MICROCOMPUTER/LAN ENVIRONMENT**	
1.	Site visit and information gathering	LAN/PC Manager
2.	Development of floor plans/PC locations	LAN/PC Manager
3.	Determine order volume	LAN/PC Manager
4.	Place orders	LAN/PC Manager
5.	Delivery/staging of computers	Vendor
6.	File server configuration	Technical Specialist
7.	Microcomputer/printer installation	Technical Specialist
8.	Acceptance testing	Technical Specialist
9.	LAN ID assignment/communication	Security
10.	End user training	Training

Timeline columns: Nov (20/27, 30), Dec 1995 (4/11/18/25, 28/27/26/25), Jan 1996 (1/8/15/22/29, 24/23/22/21/20), Feb (5/12/19/26, 19/18/17/16), Mar (4/11/18/25, 15/14/13/12), Apr (1/8/15/22, 11/10/9/8), May (6/13/20/27, 7/6/5/4), Jun (3/10/17/24, 3/2/1/0), Jul (1/8/15/22/29, -1/-2/-3/-4/-5), Aug (5/12, -7/-9)

213

F I G U R E 31 (Continued)

Comprehensive System Conversion Timeline (page 2)

#	TASKS	RESPONSIBLE
D	**VOICE NETWORK**	
1.	Determine voice network plans	Telecommunications Mgr.
2.	Develop system circuit/hardware orders	Telecommunications Mgr.
3.	Place order for facility/hardware	Telecommunications Mgr.
4.	Install/test voice circuit	Vendor
5.	Program PBXs for network dialing	Telecommunications Spcist.
6.	Training/communication	Training
7.	Communication of system availability	Telecommunications Mgr.
8.	Activate network dialing	Vendor
9.	Plan programs/grade changes	Telecommunications Mgr.
10.	Conduct IVR programming	Telecommunications Spcist.
11.	PBX programming for call routing	Telecommunications Spcist.
12.	Network activation	Vendor
E	**DATA NETWORK**	
1.	Determine network configuration	Network Manager
2.	Determine mainframe requirements	Network Manager
3.	Develop hardware/circuit order	Network Manager
4.	Place orders	Network Manager
5.	Install circuits/hardware	Vendor
6.	Configure hardware for LAN-LAN conctv.	Network Specialist
7.	Test LAN to LAN connectivity	Network Specialist
8.	Install serial circuits for ATMS	Network Specialist
9.	Install serial cables for controllers	Network Specialist
10.	Place host order requirements	Network Manager
11.	Activate LAN to LAN usage	Vendor
12.	Place order to cancel existing circuits	Network Manager
13.	Connect serial cables for hardware	Network Specialist
14.	Activate data communications	Vendor

FIGURE 31 *(Concluded)*

Comprehensive System Conversion Timeline (page 3)

#	TASKS	RESPONSIBLE
F.	Mainframe	
1.	Preplanning sessions	Coordinator/Host
2.	Determine system conversion date	Conversion Coordinator
3.	Duplicate conversion tape order	Conversion Coordinator
4.	Complete project plans/timelines	Conversion Coordinator
5.	Kickoff meeting	Conversion Coordinator
6.	Product conversion analysis	Product groups
7.	Test report receive/review	Product groups
8.	Corrections/changes	Product groups
9.	Operational work flow/procedures	Operations groups
10.	Final test reports review/approval	Product groups
11.	Freeze on host system changes	Host
12.	Walkthrough/cutover planning	Conversion Coordinator
13.	Conversion weekend	Host
14.	Cutover	Host
15.	Month end processing review	Conversion Coordinator
16.	Stabilization	Conversion Coordinator
17.	Process termination	Conversion Coordinator

1. Cabling.
2. Telephone/network installations.
3. Microcomputer hardware/software, local area network, and data network installation.
4. Platform and teller software system installation.

Cabling

Cabling requirements are determined by the site survey and floor plans obtained early in the process. From these, blueprints and diagrams of cable locations are drafted for the newly acquired organization. With this information an order is placed with the vendor who does the cabling and wiring. After the date has been established, cabling can commence. Depending on the size and complexity of the site, cabling requires anywhere from one to three weeks. This part of the system conversion must always occur prior to the installation and activation of any other technical equipment. It is important that the cabling process be well managed so that problems do not arise that could cause difficulties later at the cutover of the system conversion.

The process of managing cabling involves three basic phases:

- Coordination of equipment delivery and start-up.
- Midpoint inspection and status update.
- Final inspection and acceptance.

Coordination of equipment delivery and start-up. At this stage the individual responsible for managing the cabling (usually from information systems) must verify in person or through local on-site representation that the cables and other equipment (data rack) have been delivered and are ready for installation. Determination that the cables are on site and ready as outlined in the plan is very important, if not critical, to all other technical installations. If the cables are delayed, everything following cabling will be delayed. Clearly, this must be avoided at all costs. Once the equipment is verified and the cables are ready this portion of the management is completed.

Midpoint inspection and status update. The midpoint inspection is designed to check the progress of the cable installation and to determine if it is on schedule. This is a preventative measure, in that if cabling is running behind and may delay completion and acceptance, an opportunity exists to correct the situation before it is too late. Again a delay in the final completion and acceptance will push back all other functions behind it, thus jeopardizing a smooth conversion or the cutover date itself.

Final inspection and acceptance. This phase of management occurs once the cabling has been completed. At this time cables should be tested for connectivity and a review of the labeling and coding of all cables should take place. The neatness and acceptability of the labeling and coding will provide for a much smoother implementation of the local area network and end-user system. To that end, the individual responsible for the cabling installation should physically walk around and inspect the labeling and coding.

Cabling should commence in week 19 according to the timeline template previously developed. Obviously this requires that site surveys, floor plans, and ordering all occur prior to this time. Once the cabling has been completed, any of the other technical installations can occur. For this reason it is important that cabling be done as soon as possible.

Telephone and Voice Network Installation

The telephone system and dedicated voice network (if applicable) should be installed immediately following the completion of the cabling. Cabling provides both voice and data cabling and will furnish the necessary groupwide connectivity. The steps involved in the installation of the telephone should follow the recommended time prior to cutover for all elements. In this way planning for training can occur. The telephone and voice network installation consists of the following activities and time required prior to cutover:

Activity	Weeks
Delivery and installation of PBX	13
Telephone station reviews/programming	12
Install voice circuit hardware/circuits	12
Telephone handset/number placement	12
Program PBXs for site connectivity	12
Activate phone systems/voice network	10
Voice response system programming	1
Other voice network programming	1
Activate IVR and other systems	0

Each of the above installation activities are presented in detail in the following pages. As noted, the telephone and voice network system are installed and activated well in advance of the actual cutover. In other words, the goal is to establish the communication system early enough so it can be used during the system conversion process, thus facilitating communications while minimizing costs. In addition this provides the acquired bank's employees with the maximum time prior to cutover to get used to the telephone system and be confident in its use before cutover.

Delivery and installation of the PBX. The PBX is the telephone switch hardware that drives the telephone system. Not all banks have this technology. However, the trend in the industry is toward proprietary systems unique to the entire organization. It is probable that an acquiring bank will have this type of system. A determination is made in the preparatory phases of what type of system is needed, taking into account the size and location of the acquired bank. In some cases the new branch can be connected by an off-premises exchange (OPX) system, which is connected directly to a PBX at the acquiring bank site. Since a PBX installation is likely, our focus will be directed to requirements for a PBX installation. When the PBX is delivered, it generally can be installed and tested within a week. This will be done by the system provider and will require space in the equipment room for installation.

Telephone station reviews and programming. Station reviews can be conducted any time before the placement of the handsets. The purpose of the station review is to develop the flow sequence of calls within departments and facilities. This includes the number of rings that occur before a call transfers automatically into voice mail, establishing call pick-up zones, establishing call hunt patterns, determining the maximum number of hunts before the call terminates at the switchboard, and establishing revert patterns from voice mail. This is an extremely important process, and whatever is set up should conform to the overall bank philosophy or policy governing the use of the telephone system. In other words, if the acquiring bank has a standard that calls automatically transfer into voice mail after three rings, the new facility should not set up the system to transfer after four rings. The station review process involves face-to-face meetings with department managers and staff. Station review documents (as shown in Figure 32) are completed by the telecommunications specialist for the bank and/or the telephone system vendor, on a one-for-one basis and compiled into programming documents. The next step is to use the worksheet documents to program the telephone to respond in the manner determined during the station reviews. Again, the station review process can occur almost anytime. However, programming cannot be completed until the PBX has been installed and is active.

Install voice network hardware and circuits. After the PBX has been installed, the voice network can be installed and connected. The voice network hardware and circuits provide the dedicated pathways for internal intra- and interbank communications. The network requires dedicated circuits to be installed from the new branch location to the existing bank office to establish the connectivity. However, hardware is also required to permit this type of connectiv-

F I G U R E 32

Station Review Worksheet Document

EMPLOYEE NAME	PHONE NUMBER	DEPARTMENT/ LOCATION	HUNT TO NO.	PICKUP PHONES	REVERT TO VOICE MAIL		NUMBER OF RINGS
					Yes	No	

ity. CSU/DSUs typically are required for integrated service digital network (ISDN) circuits to be installed. These must be installed at the branch location and the connection point to the acquiring bank. CSUs/DSUs are generally installed with the circuit or facility. This should occur immediately following PBX installation.

Telephone handset/number placement. The placement of telephones involves physically setting the new telephone hardware on each desk at which it will be used. This should occur immediately following installation of the PBX. Telephones will be connected to the cable location installed earlier, which will provide access to the PBX as well as to the voice network (if available). Once the phone is installed, it should not be used until training has occurred. Furthermore, the programming from the information developed in the station reviews must first occur. Finally, the actual telephone number (new) must be determined and documented. This is obtained from the telecommunications specialist for the bank. A list of new numbers is created for the new locations acquired, and is incorporated into the programming of the PBX from the station reviews. The listing of new telephone numbers is then communicated throughout the organization prior to activation.

Program PBXs for site connectivity. PBXs are computers. As such they must be programmed to perform in the manner desired by the bank. When one PBX is connected to another PBX (different locations) via a digital voice network, connectivity does not automatically happen. Telephone numbers and tables must be updated to permit communications between the two sites. This involves programming of the PBX to activate communications between the sites. This programming should occur at the same time as programming resulting from the station reviews occurs. When complete, the telephone system and voice network is ready for activation.

Telephone and voice network activation. Upon completion of all programming, the system is ready for activation. At this point the newly acquired branches will likely have two telephones at their desks, the new handsets and the existing system. Activation of the new telephone system should not occur until training has taken place. This was discussed under the "training" nonsystem function of the system conversion in the last chapter. When training has been completed and the phone number listings have been released, the old telephone handsets should be removed—gone by return of the employees to their desks. In this way employees can begin to use the telephone while the training is fresh in their mind. This should occur approximately 10 weeks prior to the system conversion cutover. In this way advantage can be taken of the new system well in advance of the cutover, when many activities will be occurring simultaneously.

Voice response system programming. If the acquiring bank has an interactive voice response (IVR) system, programming must be done to permit access to the new location's customers. This programming cannot occur until the weekend of conversion. Any changes made prior to the conversion weekend will not be effective because the acquired financial institution and its customers will still be on a different system. Plans must be made in advance, and the actual programming must be precise and occur within a short time span. The IVR system cannot be activated until cutover, because of the mainframe differences of two systems prior to this.

Other voice network programming. In addition to IVR programming, other PBX programming that can occur during conversion weekend may consist of reprogramming calls to a central call or customer service site. If the acquiring bank has a central customer service center, customer calls must be redirected to this site so that the transition is as transparent as possible to the customer. This can be accomplished through reprogramming the PBX. This, and all other programming affecting the new customer base, should occur only during the weekend of the system conversion.

Activate the IVR and other systems. After the conversion weekend, all systems will become active as of the cutover date. This is the first day of operation on the new mainframe system. At this point the IVR system should be handling calls interfacing customer information under a new host database. In addition, if a centralized call center is used, customer calls will begin to route to this center on the first day of cutover. At this point all systems are fully active and routine use can occur.

Microcomputer Hardware/Software, Local Area Network, and Data Network Installation

Cabling, which has been installed previously, not only supports the telephone system and voice network, but it also supports the local area network and data network connectivity to the host. This portion of the technical installation provides the data side of communications and access to local area network and microcomputer-based communications. All computer devices, whether dumb terminals, as with CRTs, or intelligent devices such as microcomputers, must access the host in some fashion to use the information contained in the mainframe application systems (loans, deposits, general ledger at a minimum). This is accomplished through a data network. The devices used will either be CRTs with controllers or microcomputers communicating through file servers (gateways). In addition to this the acquiring bank may also use a wide area network (WAN), which permits LAN-to-LAN communications, PC-to-PC between branches. The initial point of connectivity revolves around the cabling that was installed much earlier in the process. Microcomputers, file servers, and data networks should be installed well before the system conversion cutover. The reason for this is to permit adequate time to test, as well as practice, prior to activation. Unfortunately, the use of microcomputers and data network connectivity requires training, with more time required than for the telephone system. Microcomputers should be the next area of implementation following the telephone system, but with a short delay so that training for the voice systems is not conducted at the same time as microcomputer training. The steps in the installation process for microcomputers, LANs, and WANs, as well as the number of weeks prior to cutover, is indicated below.

Activity	Weeks
File server configuration/installation	12
Microcomputer workstation/printers	12
Router/circuits configuration installation	12
Data/WAN testing	9
Microcomputer/LAN activation	8
Remote ATM circuit installation	6
ATM software installation/test	1
SNA/WAN communication activation	0

File server configuration/installation. File servers can be built as early as possible within the system conversion process. Building the server involves setting it up to mirror what exists for the acquiring bank. Since the disciplines involved in building and configuring the file server are different from those of the telephone and voice systems, configuration and installation can occur simultaneously with that of the telephone systems. In this regard the installation of the file server should occur during week 12 (prior to system conversion cutover). One file server will be configured and installed at each new branch and will connect to the data rack already installed by the cables. File servers and LANS also require other pieces of equipment in the technical room for access by multiple employees. These include MAUs, CAUs, and LAMs. These devices should be installed at the same time as the file server.

Microcomputers and printer installation. At the time the file server is being installed, microcomputers and printers can be staged and installed concurrently. This is to make the most of the time available in the process. As this occurs, printers will also be connected to the network. This involves connections directly to cable locations previously installed, and definition of workstation to the file server and printers to workstations and servers. Testing of the workstation itself can occur after installation; however, true testing on the local area network cannot be done until the file server is installed and active. Once this is done, the workstations should be tested and accepted as functioning properly on the wide area network. This includes the ability to share files on the server as well as software sharing. Installation can be outsourced to the vendor who provided the systems. This may be advisable considering the number of systems that may need to be installed within a short span of time. It may even be a necessity so that installation does not extend beyond the time frame in which the systems should be activated.

Router and circuit configuration and installation. At the same time as microcomputer and file server installation, routers and circuits should also be installed. Typically, routers and other data network circuits are installed by third-party vendors and therefore do not conflict with existing end-user computing staff professionals, at least initially. The data network circuits are a must to provide data connectivity to key devices in the bank where mainframe access is a must. These include teller systems, CRTs, ATMs, remote processing, and microcomputer emulation. The circuits must be installed and tested. Today, these circuits would most likely be digital. However, in some cases analog circuits are still in existence, although their use is dwindling. In addition to this, however, because of the advent of local area networks, routers must be used to provide LAN-to-LAN connectivity, for further file and software sharing as well as internal communications. These devices, circuits, and testing should occur in week 12, as well, to provide as much advance time as possible for testing, utilization, training, and shake-out prior to system cutover.

Data/WAN network testing. Upon completion of the data network and routers, testing can commence to ensure effec-

tive communications. This should begin as soon as the network is installed and not later than nine weeks prior to
system cutover. Again, regardless of whether the acquiring
bank uses wide area network connectivity, it must have a
network that provides host data communications to the new
sites. It must be installed and tested early because it will be
the main avenue of data communications at cutover. Testing
should begin not later than week nine and continue to system
conversion cutover.

Microcomputer/LAN activation. Microcomputers and
LANs should be activated within approximately two weeks
after activation of the voice system. This would place microcomputer activation at approximately week eight. The reason
is to permit as much time as possible for practice on these
systems prior to the addition of any other software, such as
platform automation, which is intensive and requires much
time for training. Employees can learn their way around a
microcomputer and gain minimum competency on standard
software within six weeks, given continual practice. Adequate
time is the best safeguard that can be provided to the users.

Remote ATM circuit installation. Most banks own and
operate ATMs (automatic teller machines). Some of the
ATMs deployed by a bank may be on-site whereas others
may be stand-alone remote placements. The latter could
include supermarket locations, remote kiosks, or other locations outside of the bank building. When this is the case,
circuits are required to connect the ATM back to the closest
branch owned by the bank. Circuits should be installed and
available when the actual conversion occurs. These circuits
will likely involve modems to be installed at each site with
an analog circuit. Since the remote ATM does not require the
bandwidth of a physical branch, digital circuits will probably
not be required. In this regard a circuit needs to be installed
by the bank's telephone circuit provider. The reason six
weeks is recommended is to ensure adequate testing time,
even though the circuit will not be cutover until the weekend
of conversion.

ATM software installation and test. If the acquired bank that is acquired already owns ATMs that will continue to be used in the combined bank, a change in software will probably be required. The acquiring bank's data processor will likely use different software to drive the existing ATMs. Because of this the existing ATMs (acquired bank's) will need to be reloaded and tested with the new software. Unfortunately, this cannot occur until the weekend of the system conversion. To take the ATMs out of use prior to system conversion would have a negative customer impact. The software installation and testing will be conducted by the mainframe staff involved in EFT (electronic funds transfer).

SNA and WAN communication activation. Both SNA (mainframe) and WAN (microcomputer LAN-to-LAN) communications will become active as of the system conversion cutover. This will be coordinated in the weekend conversion activities and will involve the setup and definition of the bank's devices at the mainframe to establish the appropriate PU (physical unit) and LU (logical unit) identifications established at the host. Again, this must be coordinated with the mainframe system conversion activities over the weekend.

Platform and Teller System Installation

If the acquiring bank uses an end-user platform automation system for its personal bankers, implementation will involve coordination with the end-user system. Additionally, teller systems have moved toward microcomputer-based systems in recent years. As a result coordination of implementation with the end-user system, file servers, data networks, and training must all be considered. Both the platform and teller software systems are pervasive in that the entire function is fully performed using these software packages. This literally automates their functions and will require fairly extensive employee training. In this regard the implementation of these systems is highlighted separately in order to focus attention on the unique requirements of these systems. The process of implementation for these, if used by the bank, will include the following steps:

Activity	Weeks
Teller training PC installation	12
Platform software installation	9
Teller PC installation	1
Platform and teller system activation	0

Teller training PC installation. Obviously, moving the acquired bank's tellers from "dumb" terminals to microcomputers cannot be accomplished until the cutover, when the new mainframe (host) is in use. Unfortunately, this does not permit much time to install the teller systems to prepare for cutover and training. To accommodate this it is strongly recommended that an individual teller PC be placed at each branch acquired when the other microcomputers are installed, during week 12 (prior to cutover). In this way tellers have a practice machine to train on prior to actual installation. This workstation is not, nor can it be, on-line. It must be a stand-alone PC. Training, in this regard, can begin earlier with tellers continuing to practice until the actual cutover.

Platforms software installation. For each personal banker workstation the software can be installed during week nine. Actually the software can be staged (loaded) at the time the microcomputers are placed during week 12. If this is not convenient, it can be done during weeks nine through four. In all cases it must be available prior to platform automation training. If the software is installed at the time the workstations are installed, care must be taken to restrict access and use of the system until cutover. In most cases the security for mainframe access will be used to permit or restrict access. In this case access codes would not be provided to the new sales staff until the week prior to conversion.

Teller PC installation. The teller microcomputers cannot be installed until the weekend of conversion. The reason is that the tellers will be using the existing system until the Saturday prior to a Monday cutover. In this regard the teller's microcomputers will be installed after the branches close on Saturday. To make the most effective use of time during a busy conversion weekend, microcomputers may be placed on the floor by the teller station ahead of time. This should not be done until as close as possible to the conversion weekend because of the obvious disruption. Precision is required to install these systems in a very brief time and ensure they are operational by cutover one and one-half days later. This is critical because one of the first areas of access, postconversion, is the tellers. If these systems are not available at conversion, it could be extremely detrimental to customer confidence.

Platform and teller system activation. Both the teller and platform systems become "live" at cutover. This indicates that both personal bankers and tellers will convert to new systems. Once cutover occurs, these individuals cannot return to the prior system. It is highly recommended that the acquiring bank place experienced personal bankers and tellers at the new branches to guide the inexperienced users of the new systems during the most critical first several days.

This completes the technical installations required for an acquisition of another bank. As illustrated timing and precision are important to ensure adequate time for training and absorption of new knowledge. These technical issues will be occurring simultaneously with the overall mainframe conversion, which is outlined in the next section.

MAINFRAME CONVERSION PROCESS

The mainframe conversion process is the principal reason for the extensive timeline developed for the system conversion process. The implementation steps in the mainframe conversion process are the activities necessary to bring existing deposits, loans, general ledger, and customer record data from one system to the surviving host system. The process involves a considerable amount of communication and reliance upon the data processing department or outsourced provider of data processing services of the acquiring bank. Everything accomplished thus far has been leading to the actual implementation and has been preparatory in nature. The focus of this section is to outline the key areas of implementation in any mainframe system conversion and to identify the timing of these activities.

The implementation phase of the mainframe conversion process is concerned with the changes that must occur in order to convert the systems. No two mainframe system conversions are alike. Most outsourced data processors have defined conversion schedules, and activities (and therefore more detailed information) will be included in the process. There will be differences between mainframe system conversions depending on the data processor involved, the level of services provided, and the software used. This section of the book is not intended to be all-encompassing for every conversion. It cannot be for the reasons previously stated. However, a number of milestones are common to every mainframe system conversion. This section provides an overview of what these items are, what is involved, and approximately when they should occur within the overall system conversion process.

For mainframe system conversions, the primary purpose is to convert existing information about customers and other financial information from one software package to another in a smooth and efficient manner, capturing all detail required. Mainframe conversions for financial institutions generally involve the conversion of information for systems such as (1) deposits, (2) loans, (3) general ledger, (4) electronic funds transfer (EFT), (5) customer information system (CIS), (6) safe deposit box, and (7) teller. Some organizations may have more that also require conversion, whereas some will have less. In general, however, for the purposes of this book, these will suffice as the base level of systems that require conversion. Other areas, more operational in nature, also are a part of this conversion. These include network, remote item processing, and security, each of which is discussed separately within this section.

The predominant activities standard for each of the application areas that are involved in the implementation phase are defined below. These are the milestone activities that must occur for the cutover to take place. Every conversion will encounter these tasks.

Activity	Weeks
Application (product) mapping	20
System parameter definition	17
Conversion programming (preliminary)	14
Test reports review (preliminary)	10
Corrections and changes	10
Change programming (final)	8
Test reports review (final)	5
Test report signoff/acceptance	2
Freeze on all changes	2

Application (Product) Mapping

Product mapping refers to the process by which each application area is reviewed in terms of the differences between the two systems as well as the definition of how information is to be converted. Product or application mapping must be conducted by the appropriate product managers of both the acquiring and acquired financial institution. In addition a product representative from the data processor of the acquiring financial institution will attend. There should be separate meetings for each product area, deposits, loans, general ledger, EFT, etc. The mapping process determines how customers and accounts will be defined for movement or conversion from one system to another. To accurately bring over customer accounts to the new system, all elements and nuances must be understood so that the programmers can write the program to convert the accounts to the new data processing system and software without losing key information. These sessions are relatively detailed and intensive. For this reason subcommittees of employees must be pulled together to ensure that the right individuals are represented to define the appropriate pieces of information or make the surviving data processor aware of important issues. The goal of product mapping is to identify the right information for translating data from one system to another. In this process, interest plans, deposit codes, and other system parameters that must also be translated to the new system will be identified. The goal is to ensure that the same operations will occur for the customer accounts as in the prior system.

Application mapping should begin as soon as possible. This can be as early as 20 weeks prior to cutover, allowing approximately three to four weeks for completion. As emphasized earlier, timing of this activity is of vital importance. If there are delays, they could jeopardize the cutover date. Care must be taken by the system conversion coordinator to effectively manage this phase to ensure that the product committee members are sensitive to time frames and ensure that effective meetings are held.

System Parameter Definition

Each data processor may label this activity differently. The activity, however, is standard in that it defines the parameters for each product area within the database. These parameters establish when reports are produced, the frequency of production, and other application-related definitions. Since the acquired bank is moving to the data processing system of the acquiring financial institution, the system parameters for each application area will be those of the acquiring bank. In this regard, few or no changes may be required. In some cases, however, due to the nature of the products offered by the acquired bank, some alteration may be required. If so, it will originate in the product mapping stage. Changes in system parameters affect all accounts, therefore attention must be paid to the ramifications of such changes. Changes may require executive committee approval and advance notice to operational areas to anticipate change.

System parameter changes should begin to occur during week 17 prior to cutover but should be identified and planned for by week 14. These may or may not affect programming; however, they should be completed prior to programming in the event they do have an impact. System parameters will generally be identified by the same group or subcommittee previously involved in the product mapping phase. It will consist of the appropriate product individuals from both organizations as well as a representative from the data processor of the surviving entity.

Conversion Programming (Preliminary)

Conversion programming is the process in which the data processing provider of the acquiring financial institution begins to program the changes determined from the product mapping review. This is considered preliminary programming in that an opportunity will exist for a review of reports to determine the degree of correctness with which the new information is being processed. Preliminary conversion programming requires the most time, simply because it is the first programming effort to be conducted. Most of the issues that arise will do so during this programming effort. As a result approximately four weeks are allocated for programming during this preliminary phase.

The programmers use product mapping documents and begin to translate information into programs that will transfer the information to the new system. This effort is conducted totally by the data processing provider and should not involve bank staff. Questions may be directed to the product committees for clarification. All conversion programming is conducted in a "test" environment and not live. The reports produced will be generated from the test bank, mirroring the current system.

Test Report Review (Preliminary)

The test report review is the stage at which preliminary programming has been completed and actual reports are being produced that compare data from the old and new systems. This information should be produced not later than week 10 so that there is time for changes and discussion. The test reports produced are reviewed by the key representatives from the product-mapping phase for accuracy and to ensure that the translations are as defined. The test reports themselves will vary by data processor. This is not a parallel review but more a comparison of information to ensure that all data are brought over and being processed correctly.

During this stage issues and changes will undoubtedly be noted. As they occur, it is necessary to document the information so that the changes can be communicated to the programmers for final programming. Again, this is a critical stage. If many changes are required, it is important to identify them as soon as possible so that the programmers have enough time to make them and prepare for final test reports.

Correction and Changes

Corrections will be noted by the individuals reviewing the test reports. As indicated above, this should occur within two weeks or less from receipt of the preliminary test reports. As the changes are identified, data processing representatives provide the information to the programmers for final programming.

Change Programming

Programming will once again commence upon receipt of changes from the preliminary test report review. This change programming should begin no later than week eight prior to conversion, earlier if changes are numerous.

As the process continues, the closer to cutover the more critical is the need for precision in completion of activities. Change programming should be given approximately three weeks or less. Any deviations from this schedule could jeopardize the final test reports, which could be detrimental to the entire process.

Test Report Review (Final)

Upon completion of the final programming, the data processor should render final reports for review. This is the same type of activity as with the preliminary test report review. The difference between the two is that little time exists for changes and programming in the event the final test report review is not satisfactory. Again, the same group of key product individuals must be involved in the final test report review. At this stage it is imperative that time be allocated to address and review these reports immediately. In the event changes must still be made, there is some time built into the process for this, albeit very little. If delays are experienced in reviewing test reports and changes are then determined, it could jeopardize the cutover date. Finally, the same is true if the test reports are not delivered for review during week five. Five weeks is deemed adequate time for receipt of final test reports and review for completion of the process.

Test Report Signoff and Acceptance

When the test reports have been fully reviewed and the changes addressed, a formal signoff and acceptance should be conducted. The purpose for this is to provide a checkpoint that indicates either satisfaction or dissatisfaction with the quality of the information converted. A decision is required at this point. The system conversion coordinator, based on the review of test reports and recommendation by the product managers, should determine whether to pro-

ceed with the conversion or not. In most cases if the programming (both preliminary and final) occurred within the
recommended timeframes, there would be little likelihood
of a delay or postponement. If however, major change is
still required, the bank would be best served by delaying
the cutover, for the problems that would be created would
have too much negative impact on the customer and/or on
the bank.

If, on the other hand, everything has converted as expected, the system conversion coordinator should sign off on
the acceptance and proceed with the cutover. This should
occur no later than week two prior to cutover.

Freeze on All Changes

Once acceptance and signoff have been provided, the bank
will convert as planned. No further changes to the bank's
systems can occur between this point and cutover. For this
reason a formal moratorium is initiated on new products or
other changes. The freeze should begin immediately following acceptance and be in effect through cutover. Actually, it
is highly desirable that this moratorium continue in effect
through termination of the process simply because cleanup
work will be required following the cutover.

At this stage the bank is ready for the actual conversion
to occur. Later in this section, other aspects of the conversion
weekend will be outlined, identifying what will happen
during conversion weekend and what to expect.

REMOTE ITEM PROCESSING ACTIVATION

Remote item processing is the aspect of the conversion that
defines how incoming checks (deposits) are to be processed
by the acquired financial institution. The acquired financial
institution will have different arrangements than those of
the acquiring financial institution. These must be made to
conform during the system conversion. The conversion ac-

tivities required will depend on how work is processed for the acquiring bank. In most cases the acquiring financial institution will desire to change the acquired bank's process to that of the current provider, if other than themselves. Therefore, it is assumed that the acquiring financial institution will reroute all work for the acquired bank to its current processor.

To accomplish this, the implementation phase involves communication and coordination by the key product managers of both the acquiring and acquired financial institutions, as in the product mapping phase. The work is similar, however, there will exist other operational issues that must be accounted for. One of the major issues to be dealt with is the volume of work that will be received. A large volume can have implications for hardware, software, and other programming requirements.

Remote item processing consists of (1) check processing (POD and inclearings), (2) bulkfile, (3) exception item processing, and (4) print distribution, and possibly other operational duties such as proof encoding, research, and statement rendering. In short, this implementation addresses the complete disposition of check deposits. The process the bank must perform to effect this transition will occur within the timeline of the overall conversion. That is, the cutover date will be the date at which all item processing will be done according to the acquiring bank's procedures and format. The process is similar to that of the application systems in that definition, programming, and testing are required. The specific milestones important to this conversion are identified below.

Activity	Weeks
Information mapping	12
Host programming and set-up	9
Testing of printback/transmission	5
Code installed/cutover and activation	0

Information Mapping

Information mapping for remote item processing involves a number of activities and decisions. The purpose of this stage is to review the needs of the acquired financial institutions. It is a comparison of information processing requirements and special handling issues. It should be conducted in subcommittee sessions consisting of representation from the acquiring and acquired financial institutions, as well as the data processor and other parties to the process. The purpose is to understand the special needs that ultimately may need to be accommodated by the group performing item processing.

In most cases the acquiring financial institution's processor will have these well established. However, changes will need to be made in order to accommodate any special handlings. Additionally, the group performing items processing needs to determine the volume of work and make decisions relative to staff additions, equipment additions, or other physical changes that may be required. Since programming is a requirement, as much advance planning as possible is highly desired. The mapping stage includes determining

1. Courier arrival and departure times.
2. Volumes (peak and daily).
3. Cash letter clearing agent and deadlines.
4. Processing days.
5. Inclearings (Fed arrival times) and volumes.
6. Bulkfile volumes (daily and end of month).
7. Exception item processing of overdrafts, etc.
8. Incoming and outgoing return handling.
9. Print distribution.
10. Proof encoding locations/handling.
11. Research/statement rendering.

All of the above must be determined, at the very least, for the acquired bank's current processing. This must be understood in order to determine what changes must be made to make the transition to the acquiring bank's processor. This phase should be completed within three weeks in order to provide the information to the processor who will perform this function postconversion.

Host Programming and Setup

Once the mapping is completed programming development can be done. Programming should commence once the mapping has been completed and it is understood how processing will occur. Programming parameters need to be developed to accommodate any changes in processing. However, the actual code will not be installed until the weekend of conversion. Unlike the test bank established for the mainframe application systems, remote processing will follow a slightly different path. However, sort patterns for POD and inclearings must be provided for as well as other differences between the two organizations.

Testing of Printback and Transmission

In most cases the acquiring bank's processor will be fully established and will have been transmitting data to the host on a regular basis. In this case, ongoing use of this transmission is the true test. Printback of reports and the like also will be functional wherever it is directed today. However, the acquired financial institution may require other host-directed printing for special circumstances. This will require definition and testing so it will be ready once conversion occurs. Normally printback of reports will occur either directly to the remote processing site and then sent via courier to the appropriate locations, or transmitted to a remote printback site. If reports are transported, new courier patterns must be added to forward reports and work to the newly acquired sites. This should occur (or at least be understood and addressed) no later than week five prior to cutover.

Code Installed/Cutover and Activation

The last step prior to activation is the installation of the code developed in programming. It will account for any changes that have occurred or been determined in the mapping and programming development stages. Code installation happens the week of cutover, for processing of the first day's work on the cutover.

Remote item processing is a necessity for any bank. As with other aspects of the consolidation, it can have definite customer impact if processing is not properly completed and errors occur. For example if month-end statements are delayed by higher than anticipated volumes or a lack of preparation, the customer will be adversely affected. Time and attention must be devoted to this as any other product during the mainframe system conversion phase of implementation. The reason this is highlighted separately is that it involves some different operational activities and is a vital ingredient in a successful conversion.

SYSTEM SECURITY AND USER ACCESS

Another critical implementation phase of the system conversion is the assignment and communication of user identification codes for access to critical systems. To begin conducting business on cutover day, users must be able to access the systems now available to them. This will involve a number of considerations on the part of the security administrator for the acquiring bank. Literally every new employee from the acquired financial institution will require access to the systems to perform their jobs. As stated earlier, there is a technical aspect to the entire conversion that calls for deployment of various telephone and end-user computing systems, each of which also requires security access. This section outlines what security is required, when it should be communicated, and what issues should be considered in the process.

For most financial institutions, a minimum of five levels of security access are required:

1. Mainframe system access.
2. Local area network access.
3. Voice mail access.
4. Teller system access.
5. Electronic mail access.

Each of these must be addressed at varying times in the conversion process, depending on when they are made available.

Activity	Weeks
Voice mail user access	12
Mainframe system security ID	11
Local area network access	9
Electronic mail access	9
Teller IDs	2
Communication of mainframe IDs	1
Test mainframe user IDs	0
Mainframe user ID activation	0

Voice Mail User Access

Early in the conversion process, the telephone and voice mail systems were two of the technical features installed. When this occurred, as part of the station review process, voice mail boxes would have been built for all users. The voice mail box will immediately take messages once activated. Since the telephone system was activated early in the process, voice mail user IDs were established and communicated to all users. Typically, this is communicated at training with an initial setup that the starter password is usually the phone number of the individual. Shortly after beginning, the user should reprogram his or her password for ongoing usage. This activation of passwords would possibly be done by the telecommunications specialist for the bank and would occur at or around week 12 prior to cutover for immediate use once the system is available.

Mainframe System Security ID

Approximately midway through the conversion timeline, the security administrator for the bank must begin to build mainframe user IDs for the employees of the acquired bank. This should be done as early as possible to minimize the amount of work during the conversion weekend. To accomplish this, the security administrator must obtain a listing of all new employees who will survive the merger or acquisition. Each must have his or her position, location, and phone number determined. This can easily be prepared using a worksheet as shown in Figure 33. This document serves to define what level of security access the individuals require by nature of their position, and where they can be reached. Most mainframe systems permit advance building of IDs with an activation timer established for each. In this case activation of the IDs would not commence until the cutover. It is very important that this be accommodated, because at the time these security IDs are built systems will be in place along with the network connectivity to access the host. It would not be prudent for individuals to begin using the acquiring bank's host prior to conversion, as this would only serve to create confusion and disruption. For this reason, communication of these codes does not occur until a later date, and activation timers are used.

When the worksheet has been completed, the security administrator should build each password, indicating the ID established for each individual on the worksheet. The worksheet forms the source document for communication to the users. In most cases, the position of the individual will dictate what type of transaction access is required for his or her security ID. If this is not defined, it will be necessary to contact the staff member's manager to determine what level of access he

F I G U R E 33

Mainframe Security Identification Worksheet

EMPLOYEE NAME	POSITION	PHONE NUMBER	MAINFRAME SECURITY ID ASSIGNED	SECURITY LEVEL REQUIRED (Transaction Types/Codes)

or she should have. In any event, close control and adherence to policy is an absolute necessity in building user IDs. The goal is to make staff members immediately productive at cutover without jeopardizing security measures.

Local Area Network Access

LANs are built and activated much in advance of cutover to permit practice and acclimation to the systems. In order for users to begin accessing LAN-related systems, a user ID must be established when the system is installed and is ready for use. In this case a LAN administrator must build and define user IDs for each person into the file server for access to the system. This must occur on approximately week nine. In this way users can begin to share files, locally (within the physical office) and share software which is installed at the file server. LAN access does not permit host access, however access to the LAN will allow one to utilize emulation software to communicate with the host and function as if one were using a CRT.

Electronic Mail Access

If the acquiring bank utilizes e-mail another user ID must be established for access to this system. The security administrator or the electronic mail administrator will likely be involved with establishing this access. E-mail permits access to messages sent from PC to PC. In this regard a high degree of confidentiality must prevail and therefore the need for security. Since e-mail would likely be installed at the time of installation of the microcomputers, the user ID should be installed and communicated at the same time.

Teller IDs

If the bank uses a PC-based teller system, as is the assumption in this book, additional levels of security access will be required. Teller systems, however, since they are PC-based, will require a user ID for access to the software product alone. In addition, since the microcomputers will be networked (operate on the LAN), a LAN ID will also be required. Finally, since host access is a must, a mainframe ID will be needed as well. Unfortunately this can get quite complicated for tellers, given the amount of security and user IDs required. Furthermore, since the teller system cannot be accessed until conversion, these user IDs cannot be communicated until shortly before conversion. The LAN ID can be built in advance, as can the mainframe ID, but the communication of these IDs should occur no sooner than two weeks prior to cutover.

Communication of Mainframe IDs

Mainframe IDs should not be communicated until one week in advance of cutover. Using the mainframe security identification worksheet (Figure 33), the security administrator would simply call each user informing him or her of their new password. Since the voice mail and telephone system is already active by this time, leaving the user ID on voice mail is secure and will suffice for communication. Individuals should be checked off of the list as they are informed. This approach is preferred to mailed communication of user IDs. Mailed communication can be opened by anyone and does not guarantee that the intended individual will look at it on a timely basis.

Test Mainframe User IDs

Mainframe user IDs should be tested on a random basis, if possible, prior to usage. This can be done by the security administrator using the IDs assigned on the day they become live, which is usually the Sunday prior to a Monday cutover. In this way if there is difficulty with access, problems can be resolved prior to the start of business on Monday. Another method of testing is to require a few users to come into the bank on Sunday and attempt to access the host. This is test enough of access. In all cases, Sunday testing prior to the start of business on Monday is highly recommended. At the very least, this affords some time in the event of problems so that they can be resolved before chaos occurs.

Mainframe User ID Activation

The activation of all user IDs should occur on the Sunday prior to Monday's cutover. For all practical purposes activation is on cutover Monday because that is when most people will use the ID. To address questions or concerns that will arise with system access, a user "hot line" should be established whereby individuals can call the security administrator directly if they experience any difficulty. Remember, if users cannot access the system, they cannot perform their jobs, which could translate into poor customer service. In addition, users will be nervous and will forget passwords, will not have access to the level of security they were used to, or will experience difficulty getting into the system. When this occurs, a telephone hot line will enable quick resolution and virtually uninterrupted functionality.

System security will be very busy shortly before and during the week of conversion. The bank should be prepared for an influx of questions surrounding the assignment and usage of security IDs. It is very important that the bulk of building the system security IDs occurs as much in advance as possible to avoid additional work at a time when many other activities will be occurring.

CONVERSION WEEKEND WALKTHROUGH PLANNING

Shortly before the conversion weekend, it is prudent to conduct a meeting to determine what will occur. In a system conversion of this magnitude, a number of activities will occur within a very short time frame, which will require much coordination. To ensure that all players know what will occur, a meeting will greatly increase the odds of a successful conversion weekend and cutover. The system conversion coordinator should establish the date of the walk-through, which should be no more than a week before conversion weekend. A meeting agenda should be developed to include the following information:

1. Listing of activities occurring over the weekend.
2. List of individuals required to be on-site/when.
3. Assignment list of duties for individuals on-site with procedures.
4. Weekend call list of all critical personnel.
5. Other events/procedures that must be performed prior to or during the conversion weekend.

The meeting should review each item on the agenda, in detail, to deal with all questions or concerns about the completion of the activity. If changes are to be made, they should be done at the walkthrough meeting. This meeting is critical to the success of the conversion weekend. Considering the large number of activities occurring, coordination and planning are of utmost importance. Each of the items in the agenda is discussed below.

Activities Occurring over the Weekend

This will include a list of the activities that will be performed over the conversion weekend. A detailed list of the most typical events occurring is found in the next section.

Individuals Required to Be On-Site and When

Conversion weekend will require some individuals to be on-site throughout portions of the weekend, and in some cases for the entire weekend, to perform various functions for testing or otherwise ensure a smooth transition. During the walkthrough, these individuals must be identified and communicated with to ensure that they know to be on-site and when. This list should be distributed to the system conversion committee as well as to the mangers of these staff employees. The work required will relate directly to the activities identified in the next section.

Assignment List of Duties and Procedures

Detailed procedures must be developed and given to the individuals who will be on-site during the conversion weekend. These procedures must also be thoroughly explained. Procedures do not have to be voluminous, nor should they be. For each job to be accomplished, a one-page document will suffice for clear presentation of steps. Of course, all of this information must be developed in advance to adequately prepare and communicate the events of conversion weekend.

Weekend Call List of Critical Employees

A weekend call list should be prepared with the name, home phone number, pager number, car phone number, or other number at which an individual can be reached during the weekend. This list should be compiled by the system conversion coordinator and distributed to all conversion committee members, senior management, data processor, and other pertinent individuals. Instructions should indicate that individuals on the list remain accessible throughout this weekend in the event a call is necessary.

The list of employees to be considered "on call" for this list should include

- System conversion coordinator.
- All system conversion committee members.
- Data processing staff (key areas).
    - Remote processing.
    - Application systems.
    - Security.

- Acquired bank product specialists.
- Telecommunications specialist.
- Security administrator.
- Conversion sponsor and/or CEO.

The list should be distributed sparingly because it will contain confidential phone numbers.

Other Events/Procedures Required Prior to Conversion

During the walkthrough it is necessary to identify other procedures or actions to be taken immediately prior to the conversion weekend which are critical for the timing of events to come. This would include procedures such as

- When tellers must cut off their work on Friday/ Saturday.
- What on-lines will be available and for how long on Saturday and Sunday.
- When the actual merger/conversion process begins.
- Availability of ATMs and timing.
- Availability on Sunday as a combined bank.
- Will tellers be operating on or off-line for Saturday.

These areas are important for the smooth coordination of events over the weekend. There likely will be others, depending on the conversion. However, the items listed provide a basic list from which to start.

CONVERSION WEEKEND ACTIVITIES

Conversion weekend, as one might guess, will be filled with activity. Because of the number of activities and the fact that locations are generally closed on Sunday, weekends are usually chosen for conversions. In addition, conversion efforts will continue through the night until all systems have been effectively converted. In this regard, it is important to have a clear understanding of the activities that typically occur over the weekend. A general acquisition/merger conversion, as defined in this book, includes the following weekend activities:

1. Teller microcomputer system installation/testing.
2. Mainframe security user ID testing/activation.
3. Host conversion programming.
4. IVR programming and activation.
5. Voice network programming for central call center.
6. ATM software installation/activation.
7. Remote items processing code installation.

Teller Microcomputer System Installation/Testing

As indicated earlier, the teller system cannot be installed until the bank closes on Saturday and balances. After this occurs, the prior system will be replaced by the new teller PCs. These must not only be installed but activated and tested to ensure functionality. For this reason outside contract installers may be required to perform the work in the available span of time. Systems must be functional by Monday morning or Sunday, if the bank has Sunday hours. It is strongly recommended that teller supervisors come in on Sunday morning to test the new systems, to become reasonably comfortable and minimize any surprises.

Mainframe Security ID Testing

Testing of mainframe security IDs should be conducted on Sunday with a random list of employees and numbers. In this way problems can be corrected prior to the start of business on Monday.

Host Conversion Programming

Host conversion programming typically begins when the bank ends work on Saturday, or before if tellers are off-line on Saturday. Programming occurs with the mainframe programming staff at their site and can last throughout the night, depending on the size of the bank. This is the actual conversion from the information developed and programmed in the test bank. These programs are converted to the live bank at this time. When this is finished, the acquisition merger conversion has been completed from the system point of view.

IVR Programming and Activation

If the acquiring bank uses an interactive voice response system, it must be configured to accept calls from the new locations. Depending on how the bank channels customer calls, this may require programming of the PBX to route customer calls through the IVR system. This must occur the weekend of conversion for activation on the day of cutover.

Voice Network Programming for Central Call Center

As in the IVR scenario above, PBX programming is required during the weekend to route customer calls to a central customer service center or central attendant, if this is the method of handling customer calls. PBXs can be programmed to route the call traffic directly into the IVR or to other remote sites for handling in the normal course of business.

ATM Software Installation/Activation

Part of the conversion process will require the upgrade of existing ATMs to new software by the processor of the acquiring bank. If the acquired bank has ATMs, this must

occur during the conversion weekend to ensure uninterrupted use of the system. It should be coordinated with the
mainframe conversion programming that is occurring.

Remote Item Processing Code Installation

The code developed for the changes required by the newly
acquired bank must be installed during the conversion weekend for activation with the work received on cutover Monday. Again this should happen during the weekend to ensure
steady operation prior to the cutover.

As illustrated many activities occur during conversion
weekend. Most, if not all, are critical to the successful completion of the conversion. In this respect timing, precision,
attention, and monitoring are required of the system conversion coordinator throughout the process to ensure timely
updates of events and/or problems. This is generally a very
intensive short period of time. Given a well thought-out
walkthrough plan and meeting coupled with effective communications, the process can be very smooth producing an
uneventful conversion, which is the goal.

CONVERSION WEEK ACTIVITIES

Conversion week begins with the cutover, which actually
should occur on Sunday. The activities that will occur during
the week are for the most part normal day-to-day bank
activities. What makes the week special is the conversion of
the acquired organization, which must be reconciled to the
bank's books. In this regard, the most important test of the
effectiveness of the conversion rests with the balancing of the
accounts and reconciliation to the general ledger. To be
prepared for the events of conversion week, the bank should
establish a conversion "hot line" for problems and difficulties in any aspect of the conversion. This will benefit future
conversions if calls are documented by area and concern. As
calls are taken, they can be directed to the appropriate area

for resolution. A hot line of this sort will also provide a sense of urgency for the resolution of these key items. Conversion week activities can be grouped into three parts, (1) system access and functionality, (2) balancing and reconciliation, and (3) operational work flow. These three areas define how effective the conversion and the prior work were performed.

System Access and Functionality

On the first day of cutover when the bank opens (usually Monday), staff employees should immediately determine if they can access the host and perform regular duties. The timely receipt of reports and the normal ability to access customer data are the most immediate tests of the technical aspects of the conversion. In addition access to systems through user security will be another test of the effectiveness of the conversion. Customers can also assess effectiveness through access to ATMs, IVRs, and general communication to the bank's support areas. These items will be determined almost immediately. The number of calls received regarding the level of functionality is a good measure of the adequacy of the technical setup of the conversion.

Balancing and Reconciliation

The status of balancing and reconciliation is not generally known until the second day of conversion week, Tuesday. The reason is that the work for Monday will not be balanced until the next day. As stated earlier, this is the primary test of the effectiveness of the conversion. If the application mapping was properly done, balancing and reconciling should be uneventful, with minimal rejects. If, on the other hand, this was not effective, difficulty in balancing will immediately occur and reconciliation will not be possible. If this happens, immediate attention must be devoted to understanding the nature of the rejected items. Are they rejecting due to procedural misunderstandings or programming issues. The cause is important so that efforts can be undertaken to correct the source of errors. Otherwise, the volume of rejects could snowball and cause considerable extra work to keep up. Balancing and reconciliation are critical to the bank's livelihood, and therefore cannot be impeded. Conversions and mergers can result in overnight growth in volume, which can highlight poor procedures, poor or inadequate training, inadequate product mapping, programming errors, or any number of problems. Attention must be devoted to addressing this issue immediately because the impact on the bank could be substantial. Close attention should be given this aspect of conversion week, with additional staff prepared to get involved if needed.

Operational Work Flow

Another test of conversion effectiveness is the flow of work. If bank employees are receiving reports and other documents on time, it is an indication that work flow activities were properly documented and training properly done. Sometimes an improper flow of work is not readily evident. For this reason, continued meetings should occur to assess the flow of work and determine if any deficiencies exist. Flow of work includes remote item processing. In this regard, the lateness of work arriving to the remote processing site from proof locations, delivered via courier, should be evaluated. Work flowing to clearing agents and posting is also a concern.

Daily Status Meetings

Ongoing meetings of the conversion committee are necessary to review progress during and following conversion week. These are normal system conversion committee meetings, however, the frequency with which they occur is accelerated. For example, during the week of conversion a brief status meeting should be conducted every day, late in the afternoon, to check progress in the three areas identified.

These daily meetings can be conducted face-to-face or via teleconference, whichever is more convenient, given the amount of work occurring. The daily meetings should continue as long as necessary. If few or no problems arise the following week, only one committee meeting need be held.

The format for the daily meetings during the week of conversion will be somewhat different than the standard conversion committee meeting and should focus on key areas of attention or "vital signs" of the conversion progress. The meeting format should follow a status check on each of these vital signs. The agenda of "vital signs" that should be reviewed each day includes

1. Balancing status of key application accounts:
   a. Cash, deposit, loans, etc.
   b. Emphasis on (1) date last balanced, (2) volume of incoming rejects, (3) volume of outstanding items.
2. Review of reconciliation of accounts to the general ledger.
   a. Emphasis on last reconciliation date and open items requiring research.
3. Daily work receipt.
   a. Review of receipt of reports, notices, and statements as planned.
4. Items processing.
   a. Time of receipt of work to the remote site.
   b. Time work sent to the clearing agent.
   c. Number of rejected items from incoming volumes.
5. System availability.
   a. On-line availability.
   b. System uptime and accessibility.
6. Security.
   a. Access to information problems/concerns.

7. Operational.
   a. Access to customer service issues/concerns.
   b. Delays in call answering or telephone issues.

The meeting should be as brief as possible because of the quantity of work people are performing. It should be approximately one hour. If numerous problems are being experienced, meetings could extend beyond this time. Should this begin to occur, the specific area affected should break off into a subcommittee or task force focusing on the issue until resolved. In all cases the system conversion coordinator should facilitate each meeting and encourage communication and a sense of urgency for resolution of issues. If the process is relatively uneventful, daily meetings should discontinue, and follow-up meetings should occur until process termination. This last phase will be described in more detail in the epilogue of this book.

SUMMARY

This chapter has focused on pulling together the efforts previously undertaken in completing the conversion. The implementation phase is concerned with actually completing the various activities, installing the systems and coordinating the system conversion effort through the conversion weekend and week of conversion. The process of implementation is broken down into categories of emphasis, to better understand and manage the complexities of executing the system conversion. The conversion of the technical systems begins the implementation process. Technical installations such as cabling, telephone systems, end-user computing systems, and the voice and data network are installed well in advance of the cutover. The reason is to permit as much time as possible for practice of using such systems so that training does not occur simultaneously for all technical systems. Some systems, such as microcomputer and local area network installations, demand practice time to gain proficiency.

This is vital in the conversion process, for if personal bankers are to rely on the personal computer to perform their daily functions using a platform automation system, they must have time to become comfortable using it. There will never be large blocks of time; however, if the installation is timed properly, ample time will be afforded these individuals to become comfortable with a system prior to learning more complex systems. Other areas of installation for telephones and networks should occur as much in advance of the system cutover as possible to allow time for "shake out" and absorption of information. In this way the technical architecture, which provides the highway system for delivery of information, will be in place well before the conversion occurs, so as not to distract employees from critical activities during the conversion weekend.

The mainframe system portion of the installation was also discussed. It is the core reason for the system conversion process to take place. The mainframe process of implementation is concerned with application and product mapping, leading to system parameter definition and ultimately to programming. These steps lead to the delivery of test reports, which are used to determine whether the product mapping effectively addressed all issues and differences in the two systems. Test reports are vital to the success of the overall system conversion. The timing of generation and receipt is critical to meeting the conversion cutover deadline. Late test reports could either cause the cutover date to be delayed or create a problem-filled conversion. In short, test reports are on the critical path for successful and timely implementation of the conversion.

Remote item processing and security concerns are separate functions apart from mainframe implementation processes. The reason is the critical nature of the activities involved as well as the fact that they do not directly relate to application mapping, programming, or test reports. In the case of remote item processing, other activities are involved that will culminate in programming but are more focused on the movement and processing of checks, from proof encoding through delivery to the clearing agent and ultimately to transmission. Programming required to adjust the item processing software to take into account different sort patterns and other special needs that will arise as a result of the business combination. Security, on the other hand, must be addressed early in the process so that user definitions are built for usage once the cutover occurs. This process requires organization and planning to ensure that users ultimately have access to the systems they need at the time they need them. Security access may not be as task or activity intensive. However, the impact on the successful implementation of the conversion can be considerable. If users cannot access the systems they need to do their jobs on the day of cutover, disruption will result in negative impact on the customer.

The last portion of the chapter focuses on the preparation for the system conversion weekend, conversion weekend activities, and conversion week itself. A conversion walkthrough is highly recommended to understand the events, changes, and activities that must occur as a result of the conversion. This will prepare individuals for these events and ensure adequate communication to key individuals as needed. The activities surrounding conversion weekend are intensive and need to occur within a very tight time span. In this regard, coordination and communication are very important. It is also important to understand what will occur at what time. One of the major activities over the weekend is the conversion programming. This culminates in a converted system, generally being cutover by Sunday morning.

Conversion week begins with the cutover on Monday. At this point communication shifts to "hot lines" and daily meetings to address key performance issues. Daily meetings are conducted as status checks to the "vital signs" of the conversion process. Vital signs include balancing and reconciling as one of the key tests that indicates the quality of the conversion process. In addition, work flow and system use and availability are other areas of concern once the conversion takes place. Daily meetings should be conducted during the first week until it is established that everything is functioning as required. If problems are experienced, these meetings should continue as long as necessary.

Epilogue

The last phase of the system conversion process involves follow-up and termination of the process. In order for this to occur there must be a formal acceptance before the process can end. When the conversion week has ended, if issues of concern are minimal, the next milestone should be to successfully pass month-end processing. The system conversion process should not end until a month end has passed. The final conversion test is to see how well the combined entity performs with month-end processing.

After completion of the conversion week, the system conversion coordinator should schedule the next formal system conversion committee meeting for the following week. The purpose of this meeting is to review and document outstanding issues and prepare for month-end processing. If month end is not close, weekly meetings should continue until month end is complete. When month-end work has been processed, the next committee meeting should focus on the results. This is a critical time, in that month end can have significant impact on customers as well as the bank. The issues surrounding month end should be documented and emphasis and urgency placed upon their correction. If the month-end issues are significant, weekly meetings should continue until the problems are resolved, possibly keeping conversion process intact until another month end has occurred. If, however, month-end processing was uneventful, with processing occurring as planned, the system conversion process is complete. At this juncture the system conversion coordinator should prepare a formal acceptance document recommending termination of the system conversion process. Approval of the acceptance document must be unanimous, signed by all members of the system conversion committee. The system conversion coordinator should be the last to sign, and the document presented to the conversion sponsor for final approval. The conversion sponsor, other senior managers as well as the CEO should review it. Once it is accepted, the document is returned to the system conversion coordinator for inclusion in the conversion workpapers. This, along with any outstanding issues, are the final documents included in the workpapers. Outstanding issues that remain unresolved are distributed to the operation responsible for their completion. At this point the system conversion process is terminated.

The success or lack thereof of the overall system conversion is the result of organization and adherence to a formal process that defines and identifies what needs to be accomplished. The steps, processes, activities, and organization outlined in this book have been used many times with much success. The detailed phases outlined in this book are a compilation of a number of years of direct experience converting and merging banks, as well as the experience and knowledge gained from adverse circumstances that have caused conversions to be other than expected. System conversion is a very pervasive, demanding, and all-consuming process that demands urgency, planning, organization, but most of all coordination and execution. Managing to a timeline permits very few avenues for deviation, especially when critical functions must be performed. Given the direction of banking in this country, in the years to come system conversions resulting from mergers and acquisitions will most certainly become the norm. The already rapid reduction in the number of independent banks in the United States today is clear evidence of the direction we are heading at the present time. The financial institutions that plan growth through acquisition and merger would do well to place heavy emphasis on their ability to plan, organize, control, and execute timely and efficient system conversions to preserve their competitiveness for the future. The steps and processes outlined in this book hope to provide the reader with the organization and understanding necessary to be a competitor in this arena, and a participant in the changes to come in U.S. banking.

Bibliography

Belasco, Kent, *Bank Systems Management*. Chicago: Probus Publishing Co., 1994.

Kraemer, K., King, J., Dunkle, D., & Lane, J. *Managing Information Systems: Change and Control in Organizational Computing*. San Francisco: Jossey-Bass, 1989.

Lewis, James P. *The Project Manager's Desk Reference*. Chicago: Probus Publishing, 1993.

Tapscott, Don and Caston, Art, *Paradigm Shift, The New Promise of Information Technology*. New York: McGraw-Hill, 1993.

Tinnirello, Paul C., *Systems Management, Development and Support*. Auerbach Publishers, 1992.

Umbaugh, Robert E., *Handbook of IS Management*. Auerbach Publishers, 1991.

INDEX

List of Books
Managing Bank Conversions

TECHNOLOGY IN BANKING

Creating Value and Destroying Profits

Thomas D. Steiner and Diogo B. Teixeira

Technology in Banking evaluates the current technology available to bankers and outlines the direction and scale of future technology. It provides market share data on dozens of businesses in which current technology is being used.

ISBN: 1-55623-150-4 $60.00

BANK SYSTEMS MANAGEMENT

The Project Management Guide to Planning and Implementing System Installations, Conversions, and Mergers

Kent S. Belasco

Bank Systems Management can help readers successfully bring a project to fruition. Whether an institution faces changes because of mergers, conversions, or progress, this guide provides the tools to help make systems changes effective and profitable and, at the same time, keep them behind the scenes.

ISBN: 1-55738-380-4 $62.50

STRATEGIC SYSTEMS PLANNING FOR FINANCIAL INSTITUTIONS

Using Automated Solutions and Technology for Competitive Advantage

Geoffrey H. Wold & Robert F. Shriver

Strategic Systems Planning for Financial Institutions was developed as a guide for the non-technical manager to create a strategic vision for information systems and technology investments. Readers will find information which covers the entire technological planning process.

ISBN: 1-55738-339-1 $60.00

BANK MERGERS, ACQUISITIONS, AND STRATEGIC ALLIANCES

Positioning and Protecting Your Bank in the Era of Consolidation

Hazel J. Johnson, Ph.D.

Whether large or small, bankers need to assess their needs and plans for the future. Mergers and acquisitions affect every financial institution in the banking system. *Bank Mergers, Acquisitions, and Strategic Alliances* reviews the process involved for banks facing any scenario caused by M&A activity.

ISBN: 1-55738-746-X $65.00

THE IRWIN PROFESSIONAL COMMUNITY BANKER Journal

The Irwin Professional Community Banker is exactly what the name suggests, a journal created for community bankers by community bankers. It spotlights a different topic in each issue that directly impacts your institution, such as branches, technology, management tools, and the people factor. *The Irwin Professional Community Banker* tackles the strategies that are essential to staying competitive and moving ahead in today's volatile banking industry.

A Quarterly Journal by Community Bankers, for Community Bankers.

Order #**CMBK** $225.00 per year